JOSEPH AND MARY

THE KEEPERS
OF
THE SECRET

Elvin C. Myers

JOSEPH AND MARY
THE KEEPERS OF THE SECRET

Copyright 2010
Revised 2022

By
Elvin C. Myers

Printed in the United States of America

Acknowledgements

Everything I have learned in my lifetime, I have learned from others. I wonder if I have ever had an original thought of my own; a thought no one has ever thought before. I doubt it! I am indebted to all who have been my teachers, sharing their knowledge with me.

I am also indebted to John Paul Myers and Lynne Thomas who proofread this manuscript for me. They did a yeomen's job in making many corrections, adjustments, and offering suggestions which greatly improved the script.

CONTENTS

JOSEPH AND MARY
THE KEEPERS OF THE SECRET

Introduction

It is probably just as well that Christmas is observed only once a year. Many people go into serious debt buying gifts and spending money on entertainment. It takes some people months to pay off their Christmas shopping bills and catch up on their credit card debt. For all the celebrating, the real reason for the season is barely emphasized.

It has been the custom of fundamental Christianity to point out the evils of observing Christmas due to its pagan background. Is there anything good about the observance of Christmas? Christians who are well acquainted with the Scriptures have taken note of the amount of space the Apostle Paul devotes in his thirteen epistles to the birth of Christ. If we relied solely on his writings on this subject, we would learn nothing. We must go back to the Old Testament prophesies and to the Gospels of Matthew and Luke in the New Testament for this information.

Besides the pagan background, misinformation abounds about the birth of Christ which causes Christians to question the observance of Christmas. The misrepresentation of God's words, the fabrication of the Bible narratives and the denial of factual biblical statements go back to the Garden of Eden. From the beginning, Satan has used lying as a means of leading people astray. Man's faulty handling of the

Scriptures is both deliberate and accidental. Either way, it is wrong and unacceptable.

The purpose of this book is to give a correct explanation of the birth of Christ with the events and people involved. An accurate biblical account of how and when the Word became flesh is a beautiful and important teaching God wants us to know and understand. Only the older King James Version of the Bible was used throughout this book.

CHAPTER 1

The Paradox of Christmas

A paradox is a statement that seems to contradict itself but in reality expresses a possible truth. For example, two cards are received at Christmas time. One has a picture of a winter scene with a horse drawn sleigh and decorated homes in a rural setting and says Merry Christmas. The second card has a manger scene with the words, "They shalt call His name Emmanuel" (Matthew 1:23) and says Merry Christmas. Both cards express the happiness of the season but from such different viewpoints that one might wonder if they were for two different seasons.

The Bible presents Christ in two ways. Luke 1:68-75 presents Christ as the Savior who will come and deliver Israel from her enemies. However, Isaiah 53 presents Christ as a man who will be lonely, rejected, and killed by a horrible crucifixion by those He came to save. This is a paradox. How can Christ deliver Israel if He is killed?

Joseph and Mary are represented as being the parents of Jesus, yet the scriptures make it clear that Jesus had no human father and that Mary did not contribute anything to the physical body of Christ. God the Father created the body of Christ (Hebrews 10:5, Luke 1:35). This is a paradox.

His name was called Emmanuel which means God with us (Matthew 1:23). Yet He was subject to His parents as a child (Luke 2:51). The Ancient of days becomes an infant of time. Can God ever be subject to anyone in the human race that He has created? God can do whatever He wants for His own reasons. He was both God and man at the same time. Christ was the Creator of the heavens and the earth. He created Eve who is the mother of all living. In the process of time, a son was born of woman who was created by the Son (Colossians. 1:16; Ecclesiastes 12:1). He would be the Seed of woman, the Seed of Abraham, the Seed of Jacob, the Seed of Judah, and the Seed of David. How could one person be all these and still be Jehovah God? This is a paradox.

There is the matter concerning the tribe of Judah. God selected Judah, the fourth son of Jacob, to be the line of royal descent out of which all Israel's kings and the Messiah would come. Moses, by inspiration, wrote the historical account of the choice of Judah in Genesis 49:10. Moses also wrote Genesis 38, which portrays Judah as an evil man. Judah went shopping for a prostitute and found one, his own daughter-in-law who had disguised herself so that he did not recognize her. Out of this encounter, illegitimate twin sons were born. Moses also wrote in Deuteronomy 23:2 that an illegitimate son was forbidden entrance into the congregation of the Lord. He says it twice. The son's offspring would also be disqualified. What was to be done about such a situation? A time limit of ten generations must pass before a son from the tribe of Judah could be reinstated into the royal family. And indeed, ten generations passed (Matthew 1:2-6), and the curse was withdrawn beginning with David who became the first King of Israel from the tribe of Judah. God makes the laws and He keeps His own laws. All these things appear to be a paradox.

The genealogical records are sufficiently intact in the Bible which prove Jesus had all the credentials to occupy David's throne. In the Adamic era, He could have been born of any woman. In the post flood Noahic era, He would have to come through the line of Shem. In the Abrahamic era, He would have to be born of a Jewish woman and descend through Abraham's son Isaac and grandson Jacob. In the Jacobic era Jesus had to come through Jacob's fourth son Judah. So the lineage of kings was narrowed down to one family from the twelve tribes of Jacob, namely Judah. David was of the tribe of Judah. In Jeremiah 22:24-30, there is the account that one member of David's family by the name of Jeconiah would be by-passed thus breaking the line of royal descent. He shall be dealt with in a later chapter.

When the Lord Jesus was to appear on earth, the prophets said He would be a servant and a king. How could the same person be both? This is a paradox.

Though there is a record of the royal lineage, could the people of Israel really be sure who the Messiah was when He came? The Jewish people were promised supernatural signs, two of which were the supernatural conception and virgin birth of the Messiah. Because liberal theologians reject the supernatural, they have also rejected the conception and virgin birth as signs. The paradox is that a human child would be born and would be God. Jesus was called the Son of man yet had no human father. The Lord Jesus Christ is all the Bible says He is, whether anybody understands it or believes it. To say He is anything less than what the Scriptures say is denial of Scriptural truth and is blasphemous. We are not required to understand how the Lord Jesus became flesh but we are required to believe it. A famous preacher used to say, the prophets said He was coming; the Gospels said He has come; and the rest of the Bible says He is coming again. The Bible is all about the Lord Jesus Christ, from cover to cover. What the Bible says is what we are required to believe, nothing more, nothing less, according to the light we have.

We come now to the question of Christmas. The word is not in the King James Bible, but neither are the words trinity, missionary nor rapture, but the concepts are there and we believe them. We are not commanded to observe Christ's birth. The Jews never observed His birth. The church observes Christmas for religious reasons and the unbelieving world observes Christmas for an assortment of reasons, a chief one being monetary.

To compound the matter, the church has badly abused the observance of the birth of Christ by fictionalizing the account. More often than not, the story we have heard so often is not found in the Bible. We are duty bound to object to false teaching. We must stand without apology for the truth. What does the Bible teach about the birth of Christ with all its accompanying events? There are some things in the

Gospels that appear to be contradictions and these need to be explained. It should never be assumed that they cannot be explained or understood.

The Unscriptural Christmas Story

We have heard it often. We learned it in Sunday school and took part in plays and pageants. We see it reflected on Christmas cards. Joseph and Mary traveled from Nazareth to Bethlehem. It was a hard journey because Mary was expecting their first child almost any day. They arrived in Bethlehem and were unable to find an inn in which to stay for the night. The innkeepers told them the inns were filled to capacity and there was no room for them. One innkeeper told them they could stay in the stable area if they wished. That night Mary gave birth to the Lord Jesus Christ. Three wise men from the east saw the star announcing His birth, and rode their camels arriving at night in Bethlehem. As they neared Jerusalem they crossed over the crest of a mighty sand dune, according to many Christmas cards, and before their very eyes was the sprawling city of Bethlehem with buildings that look like domed mosques. They found and entered into the stable where they saw the Christ child. A peaceful manger scene where a few animals are kept shows Joseph and Mary watching over their newly born son. The magi set before Him gifts they had brought for Him from the east..

This story is almost total fiction. It never happened the way it's been told. In the following chapters, an attempt will be made to give the real biblical account of the birth of Christ, exactly as the Bible gives it.

CHAPTER 2

When Jesus Was Born

In the four Gospels of the New Testament, we find some accounts repeated in each one. Christ's baptism and crucifixion occur in all four Gospels. In three Gospels, Matthew, Mark and Luke, we find the parable of the sower and the beheading of John the Baptist. In two Gospels, Mark and Luke, we find the healing of the daughter of Jairus; and the birth of Christ. Only in the Gospel of John do we read of Christ's first miracle at Cana, and the woman of Samaria, and only in Luke the story of the Good Samaritan. The two accounts of the birth of Christ in Matthew and Luke are independent of each other with no hint of collaboration between the two writers. They do not contradict each other; instead, their accounts give supplementary information.

There are some things worth mentioning from these two accounts. The first concerns the person of Christ. It may be thought by some that Christ became the only begotten Son of God when He was born. John's reference to "his only begotten Son" (John 3:16) is not about the birth of Christ, but is about His resurrection. Verse 14 speaks of His crucifixion and verses 16-18 speak of belief in His resurrection. The Greek word for begotten, **monogenes**, implies born from the dead. In Acts we read, "God hath fulfilled the same unto us their children, in that he hath raised up Jesus again; as it is written in the second psalm,

Thou art my Son, this day have I begotten thee" (Acts 13:33). The Lord Jesus Christ never had a beginning; He is the eternal Son of God, the member of the Godhead who was with the Father in eternity past.

The Lord Jesus is the child born of the virgin Mary. Not all who say they believe the Bible believe He was virgin born. At the turn of the last century, it was suggested by some church denominations that Christ could not have been born of a virgin. The idea was promoted on a large scale and, along with certain denials of other statements in the Bible, became the center of argument and conflict in the mainline Protestant denominations. This and other arguments marked the dividing of liberal theologians from conservatives, many of whom later came to be known as fundamentalists. The liberals who denied the virgin birth and other major Bible doctrines published their own Bible in the 1940's. It was the work of scholars who produced a Bible version from the original languages, which reflected their own liberal doctrinal bias. Their translation, the Revised Standard Version, was attacked almost immediately for its liberal doctrinal reflection. One case in point was the translation of a verse in Isaiah. The King James Version says "behold, a virgin shall conceive" (Isaiah 7:14). The liberal translation says, "Behold, a young woman shall conceive" (Isaiah 7:14). The argument was over the meaning of the Hebrew word, virgin, which the liberals insisted did not necessarily mean virgin. It is translated "young woman" in reference to women who were not virgins in other portions of

13

Scriptures. There should be no argument. The meaning is absolutely clear. Matthew says "Now all this was done, that it might be fulfilled which was spoken of the Lord by the prophet, saying, Behold, a virgin shall be with child, and shall bring forth a son, and they shall call his name Emmanuel, which being interpreted is, God with us" (Matthew 1:22-23). Though Mary was undoubtedly a young woman, the Greek word for virgin used in Matthew makes it abundantly clear that virgin was the intent of the Hebrew word in Isaiah 7:14.

It was not the birth of Christ that was supernatural, but the conception. The birth was natural. In Isaiah 7:14 the conception and virgin birth are mentioned in one verse. Not only was Mary a virgin when the conception took place, but she remained so until Jesus was born, even though she and Joseph were married. Concerning Joseph, Matthew says "And knew her not till she had brought forth her firstborn son: and he called his name Jesus" (Matthew 1:25).

To further underscore that Jesus was virgin born, Matthew says Mary was found with child "before they (Joseph and Mary) came together" (Matthew 1:18). In verse 20, the angel clarified for Joseph that the conception was indeed supernatural. In Luke 1, an angel appears to Mary to advise her that she would be the mother of Israel's Christ. She is greatly perplexed and asks the angel, "How shall this be, seeing I know not a man?" (Luke 1:34). The angel explains that it would be the supernatural work of God's Spirit, and it came to pass exactly as the angel said. Having this information, how could anybody doubt that Christ was born of a virgin unless there is intent to disbelieve clear facts?

The virgin birth was the fulfillment of prophecy. Who told the prophet Isaiah to use the Hebrew word in question? The Holy Spirit inspired Isaiah to write it. Who told Matthew to use the Greek word for virgin? The same Holy Spirit of God who inspired Isaiah. They are one and the same Spirit. It is unthinkable that the Holy Spirit would have meant one thing in Isaiah and an entirely different thing in Matthew. In checking Matthew 1:23 in fifteen other versions of the Bible, every one of them translated the Greek word **parthenos** virgin, just like the King James Version, no exceptions.

Even Mary was perplexed by the announcement of her virgin birth. In Luke 1:26-30, the angel sent from God announced to Mary that she would conceive a son. She obviously understood that this would take place before her marriage to Joseph and therefore asks, "How shall this be, seeing I know not a man?" (Luke 1:34). The conception came to pass just as the angel said it would; she conceived by the Holy Spirit. This presents a problem because Mary knew how her pregnancy happened. However, Joseph did not. He could only have learned this from Mary for no one else knew about it.

Did Joseph believe Mary's story? Of course not. Who would believe a story like Mary's, that her conception was caused by the Holy Spirit. No such thing had ever happened since Adam was created.

Joseph would never have believed Mary's explanation except for one thing; God sent His messenger, the angel of the Lord, who told Joseph to "fear not to take unto thee Mary thy wife; for that which is conceived in her is of the Holy Ghost" (Matthew 1:20).

How many people learned of Mary's conception besides Joseph? Only Elisabeth and Zacharias might possibly have known about it. It is quite certain that Joseph was not out in the streets of Nazareth publishing the good news. Nor would Mary have been telling people, for it would have done no good for Joseph to keep silent if Mary had been informing family and friends of her conception. Their silence is understandable for the simple reason that nobody would have believed it; absolutely no one. It was an unbelievable story. It was impossible for a child to be born without a human father. To tell people Mary was pregnant before she was married would first have brought ridicule and scorn upon Mary and she would have been considered immoral. The public would have accused Joseph and Mary of violating the Mosaic Law and committing fornication. Secondly, it would have tainted the character of the Lord Jesus Christ. He was never accused of being the result of an immoral relationship or being born out of wedlock. Everybody considered Jesus to be the legitimate son of Joseph. Not only did Mary and Joseph keep the pregnancy a secret but Elisabeth and Zacharias must have also, if they knew it. They knew their son was to be the forerunner of the Messiah, and that Mary's son was the Messiah. It would have done irreparable harm to Christ's claims to be the son of God to reveal to their family and the public Mary's pregnancy. Who knew Mary had conceived this child? Luke 2:19 and 51 tells us that Mary **kept** the sayings of the wise men, and things the angel told her, in her heart and pondered them. This was her custom. She certainly told Joseph but he told no one. They were the keepers of the secret. It is highly probable that the disciples did not know it until it was revealed to the Gospel writers. They thought Joseph was Jesus' father; John 1:45. Matthew and Luke may have been the first to make known the supernatural conception and virgin birth. The scriptures that they wrote by inspiration supported their claims. It remained a secret and the Lord wanted to keep it this way for obvious reasons. The supernatural conception and virgin birth would not be revealed to the public until after the Lord had been crucified, resurrected from among the dead, and ascended into heaven. The Lord's miracles and resurrection gave credence to the supernatural conception and virgin birth. One tends to support the other. It was no accident or coincidence that the Roman government decreed that a census was necessary about the same time as Mary's pregnancy. It is not certain why the Roman government issued the decree at this time. The decree made it essential for Joseph to take Mary and go to Bethlehem to be registered for the census and taxation. Being of the royal family of Israel made it all the more imperative. The Roman government had a record of when the Christ of Israel's royal family was born, so it was twice recorded, once by Rome, and again in Israel's genealogical records. Joseph and Mary left Nazareth very soon after they were married and long before anyone would have known Mary was pregnant. It was their secret. It is usually thought they left Nazareth very near to Mary's due date. If this would have been the case, how could she have kept her condition secret? In Bible times, women often secluded themselves during the latter months of their pregnancy. If Mary had done this, it would have been a sure giveaway and people would have begun asking questions, or at least guessing. It was of the highest importance that they leave Nazareth before people knew. They arrived in Bethlehem where almost no one knew them nor cared about her condition. Joseph and Mary were living there for several months before the Lord was born, and that is what the Bible implies in Luke 2:6 where it says, "and so it was that, "WHILE THEY WERE THERE, [bold print by the author] the days were accomplished that she should be delivered" (Luke 2:6). This can only mean that it was not the night of their arrival in Bethlehem, but during the time they were living there that Christ was born, with no questions being asked by anyone. But doesn't Luke 2:5 say Mary was "great with child" when they went to Bethlehem? The KJV does indeed say that. There are several Greek words for "great" and not one of them is found in the five versions of Luke 2:5 of the Greek New Testaments checked. In checking fifteen English translations of this verse, not one of them has the word great. Two have the words "obviously pregnant" and one had "advanced pregnancy". Neither obvious nor advanced, both relative terms, are found or implied in the original language. All the text says in Greek is that she was with child. It is reasonable to conclude that Joseph and Mary went to Bethlehem while it was easy for her to travel, and it was probably during the early months of the year while her pregnancy could remain a hidden secret. It was months after their arrival in Bethlehem when Jesus was born. Did the little town of Bethlehem celebrate Christ's birth? Was it Christmas time in Judea? Did anybody notice or care? Didn't the Lord's disciples know Jesus was supernaturally conceived and virgin born? They did not. They never mention or even hint that they knew it. Like everyone else, they thought Joseph was Jesus' father. "And Jesus himself began to be about thirty years of age, being (as was supposed) the son of Joseph" Luke 3:23. The disciples, perhaps, first learned about Jesus' birth when Luke and Matthew wrote their gospels, after the resurrection of Christ. It must have come as a surprise to everyone. Alternatively, the Lord could have revealed it to the disciples following His resurrection when, according to Luke "then opened he their understanding, that they might understand the scriptures" (Luke 24:45). He could have explained Isaiah 7:14 to them.

If it be argued that the disciples would have known Jesus was supernaturally conceived and virgin born because it was recorded in Isaiah, and they had access to the scriptures, let it also be admitted that the Lord's resurrection is also recorded in the Old Testament, yet they did not believe he had risen from among the dead until after the resurrection happened and they saw Him alive. They had to believe what they saw and heard. The Lord's resurrection is mentioned in the Old Testament more often than the conception and virgin birth. Yet, they did not believe it, so why would mention of it in Isaiah 7:14 cause them to believe it?

Two men were walking along the road to Emmaus. The risen Lord joined them and immediately directed their attention to the Old Testament. "Beginning at Moses and all the prophets, he expounded unto them in all the scriptures the things concerning himself" (Luke 24:27). Surely one of those things would have been His rising from the dead. He spoke of things written in the law of Moses, and in the prophets, and in the psalms" (Luke 24:44). "And he said unto them, thus it is written, and thus it behoved Christ to suffer, and to rise from the dead the third day" (Luke 24:46). The Psalmist wrote, "I will declare the decree: the Lord hath said unto me, Thou art my Son, this day have I begotten thee" (Psalm 2:7). The apostle Paul, preaching in Antioch of Pisidia said, "God hath fulfilled the same unto us their children, in that he hath raised up Jesus again, as it is written in the second psalm, Thou art my Son, this day have I begotten thee" (Acts 13;33). Paul explained that the word "begotten" refers to the resurrection. A similar expression is found in Psalm 16:8-11 and explained by Peter when he was preaching on the day of Pentecost concerning the resurrection. The disciples believed in the risen Lord after they actually saw Him but not before. They were hard to convince. They did not know the meaning of Isaiah 7:14 about the conception and virgin birth of Christ until it was revealed to them by the Lord after his resurrection, or they learned it from the inspired writings of Matthew and Luke.

"And it Came To Pass"

"And it came to pass in those days, that there went out a decree from Caesar Augustus, that all the world should be taxed" (Luke 2:1). What days? These must be the days appointed by the Lord for His Son to be born into the world. This might be what Paul was referring to when he wrote in Galatians, "But when the fullness of the time was come, God sent forth his Son, made of a woman, made under the law" (Galatians 4:4).

In those days John the Baptist was born. He was appointed the forerunner of the Messiah. That's the subject matter of Luke chapter one. When the decree for the census came from the emperor in Rome, it is likely that John the Baptist had already been born. If this is so, then it means that Mary was already with child.

When the decree became known in Nazareth, Joseph and Mary could have quickly settled matters and quietly left town. They had a perfectly good reason for doing so; they were going to Bethlehem to be registered in the census and to pay their taxes.

It seems that it was not in Joseph's plans to return immediately to Nazareth after the Lord Jesus was born. People could have figured out when Jesus was born if they had returned right away. The time of Jesus' birth was to remain a secret. They planned to stay awhile in Bethlehem and were still there when Jesus was nearly two years old. If Joseph and Mary had returned to Nazareth with a new-born baby in their arms, people could have easily guessed about the baby, namely, that Mary must have been pregnant before she was married. Her pregnancy would have been a secret no longer. They went to Egypt and stayed there awhile, so even more time passed, and upon returning to Judea, they evidently planned to return to Bethlehem. Instead, they went back to Nazareth. Matthew 2:22 says that while Joseph and Mary were in Egypt, they heard of the death of Herod and made plans to return to Bethlehem of Judea. God warned them not to return there for it says, "being warned of God in a dream, he turned aside into the parts of Galilee" (Matthew 2:22). Nazareth is in Galilee. There was no need for the warning if Joseph had not planned to return to Bethlehem. Joseph feared returning to Bethlehem because he knew of the treachery of Archelaus who reigned in the place of his father Herod. If he had plans to return to Bethlehem, he would have needed to fear. From the time Joseph and Mary left Nazareth until they returned, about three years minimum had passed.

While they were living in Bethlehem, "the days were accomplished that she should be delivered"

(Luke 2:6). The question may be rightly asked, if they were living in Bethlehem for several months, why were they still living in the inn? An inn is a place to sojourn. The inns were temporary shelters, especially for travelers. Christ's time in this world was a sojourn. It was temporary; He sojourned here on earth. We, as believers in the Lord Jesus Christ, are doing likewise. This world is not our home; we are sojourning here; just passing through until we die or until Christ comes to take us home. Inns receive all comers. So does the Lord Jesus Christ. He receives everyone who comes to Him for salvation. Since the Scriptures do not satisfy our curiosity about all things, we have to admit we do not know why Joseph and Mary were so long at the inn. It is a guess that since Joseph was a carpenter, he could have been building a house, and have done so while earning a living doing carpentry work for other people. They were living in a house when the wise men came to visit them. It is most likely that his family living in the Bethlehem area had land there, yet strangely, no one of his family seems to offer them accommodations. Perhaps they offered land. Since Bethlehem is a small village, it is possible that there were no houses available to buy or rent. In our 21st century culture, we can go into almost any town and find a place to buy or rent, but it was probably quite different in the little rural town of Bethlehem.

Doesn't the Bible say the baby Jesus was born in a stable area of an inn because the inn was full of travelers and there was no room for any more people?

It does not say exactly that. There is a better explanation. Luke says, "And she brought forth her firstborn son, and wrapped Him in swaddling clothes, and laid him in a manger; because there was no room for them in the inn" (Luke 2:7). It is an assumption to think that Joseph and Mary arrived in Bethlehem only to find the inns filled to capacity and that they were told by an innkeeper that they could stay in the stable area of the inn. First, there is no mention of any innkeeper. The innkeeper is a fictitious invention. Second, it does not say Joseph and Mary had just arrived in Bethlehem. Third, it does not say the inns were overflowing with travelers. What it does say is that Mary gave birth to her baby in the stable area, implying that there was no room in the inn for this event to take place. They retreated to the stable area of the inn where they had been staying because there was no room inside for privacy for such an event as giving birth to a baby. Inns did not offer much privacy.

Chapter 3

Those Who Knew Jesus Was Born

From the narrative in Matthew Chapter 2, it might be supposed that no one in Israel knew Jesus had been born. When the magi arrived in Jerusalem and asked where they could find Him who was born King of the Jews, nobody seemed to know anything about it. In fact, there were actually many people who knew Christ had been born.

The magi knew Christ had been born because it was announced to them by a sign in the sky. Surely, their excitement about this would have caused them to tell everyone around them in the east that the King of the Jews had been born in Judea. They came into Jerusalem "Saying, where is he that is born King of the Jews? for we have seen his star (light) in the east" (Matthew 2:2). Surely, they told people in their homeland where they were going and why. When their inquiry became known to Herod, King of Judea, Matthew wrote that "he was troubled, and all Jerusalem with him" (Matthew 3:3). No one was able to tell the magi where to find this child. The child must have been nearly two years old when the magi came to visit, yet in all this time it seems that Christ's birth was a secret. However it only seems that way. When Herod called for a conference with the priests and scribes, they were able to tell where Christ would be born, but they were not able to tell him that His birth had already taken place. They knew where but not when.

Why is it that nobody could tell the magi where Jesus was? Had they simply forgotten? Was His birth made known, but the Jews didn't believe it? If His birth was never announced to Israel, that would account for their lack of knowledge of it.

However, that is not the case. His birth was widely broadcasted. First, Luke 2:8-20 tells of shepherds who were keeping watch over their flocks of sheep in fields near Bethlehem. An angel appeared to them with a message from the Lord. He told the shepherds that Israel's Christ had been born, where He could be found, and how they would know they found the right baby. "For unto you (the nation of Israel) is born this day in the city of David (Bethlehem) a Savior, which is Christ the Lord. This shall be a sign unto you; (that they might know for sure) Ye shall find the babe wrapped in swaddling clothes, lying in a manger" (not where you would expect the King of Israel to be born), (Luke 2:11-12).

That Christ was to be born in Bethlehem was no secret. The Old Testaments prophets knew He would be born there. Bethlehem was a very small farming village in the hills of Judea about five miles south of Jerusalem. Our Christmas cards often depict a sprawling city with domed buildings like mosques seen over the rooftops of houses, but that is far from the picture we see in the Bible. Some Christmas cards show three men (the wise men) on camels perched on the crest of a sand dune with the city spread out before them and a bright star shinning in the heavens above the city. Bethlehem is not anywhere near the Arabian Desert; it is in the mountains. Those artists who make up these scenes would do well to read their Bibles more accurately.

Bethlehem means "house of bread". Perhaps this is because Bethlehem and the area around it was a farming community. The people who lived in and around the little town were grain farmers, like Boaz in the book of Ruth, or they were shepherds like King David and the men in the narrative in Luke. According to Ezra the scribe, who led Jews back to Judea from Babylon after seventy years in exile, about one hundred and twenty three people returned from captivity and settled in and around Bethlehem (Ezra 2:21). The town is still there after more than four thousand years of history, but today it is heavily commercialized and under Palestinian control. Somewhere outside the little town of Bethlehem, Jacob the patriarch buried his beloved Rachel. The romantic story of Boaz and Ruth took place in the fields and town of Bethlehem. Ezra the scribe, Nehemiah the Persian King's cupbearer, and Jeremiah the prophet all speak of activities related to Bethlehem, and it was where David, the shepherd king was born.

A significant mention of the city is made in the prophetic book of Micah, "But thou, Bethlehem Ephrata, though thou be little among the thousands of Judah, yet out of thee shall he come forth unto me that is to be ruler in Israel; whose goings forth have been from of old, from everlasting" (Micah 5:2). Micah's prophecy says that He who was prophesied to come would be the ruler, the King of Israel, that He would come out of Judah, and that he would be from the family of David. It should have come as no surprise to the nation of Israel when Christ was born in Bethlehem. The people should have launched an investigation to determine the truth of such a highly important matter. If it be argued that they did not know Christ had been born, that is not true.

In the Gospel of Luke we read of the shepherds who were visited by the angel with the Lord's announcement of Christ's birth, "And when they had seen it, they made known abroad the saying which was told them concerning this child. And all they that heard it wondered at those things which were told them by the shepherds" (Luke 2:17-18). "Let us…go…and see", the shepherds said in Luke 2:15. Nobody else went to see. It is plausible to think that the shepherds did not tell their story just once or twice, but that they told it often all the days of their lives. After all, who could forget seeing an angel and hearing the message all Israel had been waiting for? How could they possibly restrain themselves for years to come from telling everyone of seeing Israel's Christ that night when He was born? Do we need a scripture verse to verify that this is most likely the case?

Perhaps the content of their account was what made the people wonder. Born in a stable of an inn?

Laid in a manger, a food troth for animals? Wrapped in swaddling clothes? His father, a practically unknown, lowly carpenter? How could this baby, born in abject poverty, become the Savior King of Israel? It would never get any better for this baby, for we are told the Lord Jesus had no place to lay his head all the days of His adult life on earth, (Matthew 8:20). "Though he was rich, yet for your sakes he became poor (2 Corinthians 8:9). How could one born so lowly rise to be King? This was not the entrance into the nation of Israel the Jews would have expected. It must have been that the shepherds told their story to anyone who would listen, and they told it over and over, giving every detail. Many heard that Jesus had been born in Bethlehem. The shepherds heard, believed, obeyed, praised, rejoiced and testified of Christ the Lord's birth to the inhabitants of Judea. We have to wonder, were the people not listening? Were they not interested?

The shepherds were not the only ones who saw the baby Jesus. When Mary's forty days of purification were completed according to the law, she and Joseph went to the temple in Jerusalem "to present him to the Lord" (Luke 2:22-24; Leviticus 12:1-8). The Mosaic Law had specific requirements that had to be fulfilled when the first son was born. When they entered the temple, there was a man there named Simeon with whom God's Spirit dwelt and who had revealed to him that he would not die until he had seen Israel's Christ. The Holy Spirit knew exactly when Joseph and Mary would be at the temple and brought Simeon there at that exact time. When Simeon saw the baby Jesus, he "took him up in his arms, and blessed God, and said, Lord, now lettest thou thy servant depart in peace, according to thy word: for mine eyes have seen thy salvation" (Luke 2:28-30). With his own eyes, Simeon saw the baby Jesus, He who was prophesied to be Israel's ruler, the King of the Jews. What are the chances that Simeon kept this experience to himself and never spoke of it to anyone, or did so in a rather nonchalant manner? This Spirit-blessed man must have told family, relatives, friends and anyone else who would listen that Israel's long-awaited Messiah had been born. This was exciting news. Therefore, with Simeon's eyewitness account and the testimony of the shepherds, many people in Jerusalem knew Jesus had been born in Bethlehem.

Then there was Anna. She was a prophetess of great age, a widow of eighty-four years, who spent her days at the temple worshipping the Lord in prayer and fastings. What could she have prayed about? Most likely, she prayed for the redemption of Israel. She came into the temple while Simeon was praising the Lord for the baby Jesus. She saw the baby in his arms and joined Simeon in thanksgiving to the Lord for this child. He was the hope of Anna's and all Israel's redemption. Luke says she "spake of him to all them that looked for redemption in Jerusalem" (Luke 2:38). Many Jews who came to the temple in Jerusalem, a busy place, heard that Jesus had been born. Surely word would have spread like ripples across the water.

The accounts of the shepherds, Simeon, Anna and later the magi provide enough information to tell us that hundreds, and possibly thousands in Jerusalem and Judea heard that Christ had been born. However, the announcements must have fallen on deaf ears. The quality of the Jews spirituality was very low so that they cared little for what they heard. "He came unto his own, and his own received Him not" (John 1:11). The Jews were always unnecessarily confused about who Jesus was. Some said He was the Christ. Others disagreed saying "Shall Christ come out of Galilee? Hath not the scripture said, That Christ cometh of the seed of David, and out of the town of Bethlehem, where David was?" (John 7:41-42). The Jews knew the prophecy about Christ but seemed unmoved by the announcements that He had been born in Bethlehem or that He was of the royal family of King David.

The Wise Men

Who were the wise men, called the magi? We know they came from the east. Since directions in the Bible are north, south, east and west of Jerusalem, the men came from east of Jerusalem which is usually thought to be Persia, Mesopotamia Chaldea, the homeland of Abraham when he was called by God. It has been suggested by some that the magi were Persian astrologers. One translation of the Bible calls the wise men stargazers. Many scholars, like Matthew Henry, believe they were Gentile Persian astrologers. Astrologers were men who studied the heavens and saw messages for mankind in the formation of the stars, planets and constellations. In studying the heavens, they supposedly saw a star that announced the birth of the king of Israel, and they made a long journey from the east to Judea to pay homage to the newborn king.

There is not one verse in the Bible that says these men were astrologers. That is a bad guess. In fact, they were not Persian Gentiles at all. They were Jews who were living in Persia at the time Christ was born. What interest or reason would Persian Gentiles have to seek the king of the Jews?

If we think this through in the light of the scriptures, we will know that astrology is not a scientific discipline call astronomy. Astronomy is a legitimate science. Astrology is a pseudoscience that is condemned in the Bible, (Deuteronomy 18:9-14; Isaiah 47:12-14). It did not work and even the astrologers knew it. In Daniel 2, Nebuchadnezzar, king of Babylon, had a dream. Verse 2 says he called "the magicians, and the astrologers, and the sorcerers, and the Chaldeans, for to show the king his dream. So they came and stood before the king" (Daniel 2:2). He wanted all these men to tell him what the meaning was of his dream because it troubled him greatly. If they failed to tell him the meaning of his dream, he threatened to cut them in pieces. In verse 10, "the frightened Chaldeans answered before the king, and said, There is not a man upon the earth that can shew the king's matter: therefore there is no king, lord, nor ruler, that asked such things at any magician, or astrologer, or Chaldean" (Daniel 2:10). The king suspected these men were deceivers, but here was one time they told the truth. Astrology could not be counted on to reveal anything past, present or future.

In Isaiah we read, "thou are wearied in the multitude of thy counsels. Let now the astrologers, the stargazers, the monthly prognosticators, stand up, and save thee from these things that shall come upon thee. Behold, they shall be as stubble; the fire shall burn them; they shall not deliver themselves from the power of the flame: there shall not be a coal to warm at, nor fire to sit before it" (Isaiah 47:13-15). This is God's warning of judgment to come upon Israel and the astrologers will not have the foresight to warn Israel of impending judgment, nor words to warn or deliver them. Astrology is clearly condemned in the Bible in Deuteronomy 18:9-14 and Isaiah 47:12-14. God will judge the astrologers. Why would God pronounce judgment upon these men and their practice and then use what He had condemned to announce the birth of Christ to Israel and the world? Neither by the pseudoscience of astrology nor by the discipline of the legitimate science of astronomy did the magi learn of the birth of Christ. When has the truth of God's word ever depended on science for proof of its veracity? Science is the measure of what man has learned and is unreliable. The Bible is true no matter what science says because all scripture is inspired by God who cannot lie, err, deceive nor be mistaken in any way.

The magi were Persian Jews. Why were they in Persia? They were carried there by Nebuchadnezzar and the Babylonian armies that destroyed Jerusalem, the temple and the hamlets and villages of Judea. From 606 to 581 B.C. they carried away thousands of Jews to Babylon as slaves and captives of war. The Jews were exiled to Babylon for seventy years after which time the kingdom of Babylon fell to the Medes and Persians. The new ruling world powers gave the Jews permission to return to Judea, and many Jews did. However, thousands stayed behind, having been born in Mesopotamia and were established in the way of life there. Undoubtedly, some were in poor health or too old to make the trip to Judea.

Many Jews had no desire to leave their home in the Euphrates River valley. That's where they originally came from. Be that as it may, they never forgot who they were. During the seventy years of exile from their homeland, they had the prophets Ezekiel and Daniel who ministered to them in writing. After the captivity ended, the Jews had the prophets Haggai, Zechariah and Malachi to minister to them. There was also the leadership of godly stalwarts such as Ezra the scribe and Nehemiah, the Persian king's cupbearer. The book of Esther takes place in Persia after the captivity ended. In all this time, the Jews never forgot God or His promises. The Jews were there in Persia when Jesus was born. They were there thirty some years later on the day of Pentecost in Acts 2 when Jews came from all over the Euphrates river valley. "And how hear we every man in our own tongue, wherein we were born? Parthians, and Medes, and Elamites, and the dwellers in Mesopotamia" (Acts 2:8-9).

In Daniel 9:24-25, a timetable is clearly given indicating when Messiah would appear in Israel. From the rebuilding of the wall of Jerusalem to the coming of the Messiah would be 483 years. If there is one thing the Jews can do very well, they can count, and it is possible that many of them had been counting off the years. When 483 years had passed, they were watching for some indication that Messiah had arrived in Israel. It must have been an exciting time for them as they watched for a sign. Finally, they saw the announcement in the light that appeared to them.

The assembly of wise men who came often before King Nebuchadnezzar eventually included Jews. This was intentional. Godly Jews were blessed with wisdom by the Lord and this was recognized, especially when Daniel told what the King dreamed and the meaning of it (Dan.1:4 and 20). Daniel and his three godly companions were included among the wise men. In Daniel 2 we read, "For this cause the king was angry and very furious, and commanded to destroy all the wise men of Babylon. And the decree went forth that the wise men should be slain; and they sought Daniel and his fellows to be slain" (Daniel 2:12-13). In Daniel 2:20-22 Daniel testifies about the source of true wisdom; God gives it. How has God given wisdom today? He wrote it down. His wisdom is in black and white. The Bible is the source of God's wisdom. It was God-given wisdom that saved Daniel and his friends and the false wise men at Daniel's request. These Jewish magi in the Old Testament, who had the Scriptures, were godly men who were looking for the coming Messiah, and they were the kindred of the wise men who came to Jerusalem searching for "he that is born King of the Jews" (Matthew 2:2). They did not arrive in Jerusalem asking if Christ had been born, but where. What did the magi know about the Messiah? They knew he would come from the tribe of Judah, be a descendant of King David and would sit on David's throne, and that He would be introduced by a light, a "Star out of Jacob (Numbers 24:17). Would they have been surprised to find upon arrival that not all Jerusalem was worshiping the recently born King of the Jews? Or that Herod was completely unaware of Jesus' birth? The wise men knew Christ had been born but did not know where. The scribes and Pharisees knew where Christ was to be born but did not know when. The scribes and Pharisees did not argue among themselves where Christ was to be born; they were unanimous and in perfect agreement that it would be in Bethlehem of Judea. As mentioned earlier, there was another town by the same name located in Zebulun of Galilee (Joshua 19:15). The Holy Spirit specified Judea so a mistake could not be made as to which Bethlehem was meant. After their meeting with Herod, the wise men went to Bethlehem alone. There was no escort. Amazing! The wise men's report of seeing a light should have interested the scribes and Pharisees enough to go, or at least, send someone to check and see. Herod and all the Jews in Jerusalem were troubled at the wise men's report, but seemingly not at all curious. Why was Herod concerned at all? He had been on the throne for over 35 years and was at the end of his reign. It would be many years before the new King would have been any threat or have any impact on governing Israel. Herod evidently hated the idea of anyone replacing him and jealousy became his master. It was of little interest to the people otherwise.

How did the wise men know, when they saw the child, that they were looking at the Messiah? There was no halo about his head. Did Joseph and Mary tell them Jesus was the Christ, the new born king? It must be that the magi knew who the child was because of the light that led them to exactly the right house in Bethlehem and Jesus was the only child in the house.

They rejoiced to see Him (Psalm 105:3). Were they disappointed to find Him who would be King of the Jews in such a humble abode and not in a palace-like residence? Perhaps not, for we read that they fell down and worshiped Him, and presented Him with precious gifts. As far as we know from the record, they did not honor Herod in that way when they were presented to him. The wise men might have returned to tell Herod what they found in Bethlehem, but God told them not to return to him. They left for home by a different way that did not take them through Jerusalem. If they had been in Nazareth, as some claim, they would not have needed to go home by a different way. Thus, they unknowingly avoided being accessories to Herod's wicked plan, namely, the murder of innocent children. That was one time when ignorance was a blessing.

The Star

Religion and tradition have many ideas that are completely foreign to the Bible. The problem is compounded by the careless misreading of the Scriptures. This leads to misconceptions. The problem is further complicated by improper and insufficient research that leads to unsound conclusions. Those who love the Lord and love His Word want to avoid all this and understand the Bible the way the Lord intends. To do this, trust only the Bible, rightly divide it, examine every word, verse and context, and compare scripture with scripture. Adding anything to the Bible's record is an attempt to show knowledge above that which is written. It helps greatly to have good working tools like a concordance, Bible dictionary, English dictionary, lexicons and word study books of Greek and Hebrew. The use of the old King James Version of the Bible is recommended because so many of the concordances, commentaries and Bible dictionaries are oriented to it.

The questions at hand are about the star seen by the magi. Was it a literal star? How did it announce the birth of Christ? How did it serve as a sign to the magi? How did it guide them to the exact house where Joseph, Mary and the child Jesus lived? Where was the star when the magi saw it? If the people living in Judea were unaware of it, why would that have been the case? Why couldn't the star in the sky seen by the Magi also be seen by the people in Judea? If it shined over Judah, surely many people would have seen it.

In Matthew 2, we are told the magi, known as the wise men, arrived in Jerusalem looking for the recently born King of the Jews. They knew He had been born because they said, "we have seen his star in the east" (Matthew 2:2). As mentioned before, east, west, north and south in the Bible are in relation to Jerusalem. The magi lived east of Jerusalem, namely on the other side of the Arabian desert in Persia. Does their inquiry mean the star was in the east where they lived when they saw it locally, or does it mean they were in the east looking west toward Jerusalem and saw the star over Judea? If the star appeared in Persia locally to the magi rather than to people in Judea, this would explain why people in Judea apparently did not know about it. Herod never heard about the star until the magi arrived. We gather from Matthew 2:7 that he had to ask them about what time it appeared.

It is repeated in Matthew 2:9, **"the star which they saw in the east"** (bold type the author's) and if this means they were in the east looking west toward Judea, then we have to wonder why everybody in Judea did not also see it. The wise men saw it locally in the east where it appeared.

Was what the magi saw really a star? A star is a celestial body that God created and placed in space and set on fire. Our sun is a star. Is a literal star what the wise men saw? Did God create a special star for the occasion? Some think it might have been a supernova. Supernovas have occurred at various times in history. How can one be differentiated from another so as to announce the birth of Christ or anything else? God certainly has the power to announce Christ's birth this way, but is this what He did?

The magi definitely saw something. The Greek word for star is **astera** or **astron**. In the Old and New Testaments combined these two words are used a minimum of seventy-one times. They almost always refers to literal celestial stars. But almost implies there are exceptions, that is to say, times when star refers to something or someone else. In Jude 1:13 false preachers are called wandering stars. In 2 Peter 1:19 there is reference to the day star that will arise in the heart. Job 38:7 calls angels stars, as does Revelation 1:20. In Revelation 22:16 the Lord Jesus called Himself the bright and morning star.

What did the magi see? They saw an astron, a light in the heavens. They saw the sheckinah light that represented the presence of God or God's messengers. In Numbers 24:17, we read of the promise that a star would rise out of Jacob; in other words, a light out of Israel. When Jesus ministered to the Jews, He identified Himself as the Light of the world. John the Baptist said Jesus was "the true light, which lighteth every man that cometh unto the world" (John 1:9).

The Jews were very familiar with the light that represented the presence of God. It was also the light that filled the holy of holies in the tabernacle and the temple. It was the light that Peter, James and John saw on the mount of transfiguration. Saul of Tarsus was struck to the ground on the Damascus road by this same light, which represented the presence of Christ Himself when He appeared to and spoke to Saul. It was not a faint light, but was brighter than the sun, a blinding light. It represented the glory of God. In Exodus 24 we read, "And Moses went up into the mount, and a cloud covered the mount. And the glory of the Lord abode upon Mt. Sinai, and the cloud covered it six days: and the seventh day he called unto Moses out of the midst of the cloud. And the sight of the glory of the Lord was like devouring fire on the top of the mount in the eyes of the children of Israel" (Exodus 24:15-17). The cloud that covered the mount was a glorious cloud of light that all Israel saw. It was the sheckinah light on which Israel came to depend.

It appeared to the shepherds who were watching their sheep the night Jesus was born. Did others in Bethlehem see this light? Was the light that shined upon the shepherds the light the magi saw? Most likely the light was local and not broadcast all over Judea. If people in nearby Jerusalem did not see it, then surely the magi in Persia did not see the light the shepherds saw, unless the same light appeared simultaneously in two different locations. It seems reasonable to think that if the light appeared to the shepherds without others knowing about it, it could also have appeared at a different time in a different place to the magi in Persia unnoticed by people anywhere else. In Luke 2 we read, "And, lo, the angel

41

of the Lord came upon them, and the glory of the Lord shown round about them, and they were sore afraid" (Luke 2:9). This "glory" is identified as the light of the Lord. The sheckinah light represented the presence of the angel of the Lord. Israel saw the same light upon Mt. Sinai.

The same light that appeared to the shepherds in a field outside Bethlehem was most likely the same light that appeared to a group of Persian Jews who had been counting the days, watching and waiting for the fulfillment of God's promise to Israel. The sheckinah light was a sign to the magi, the star that would rise out of Jacob mentioned in Numbers 24:17.

When the magi arrived in Jerusalem, why did they have to ask where Christ was? If they knew the Scriptures, did they not know that Micah said He would be born in Bethlehem? We can only guess, but it may be that since nearly two years had passed, He may have not been in the exact same place where He was born, and in fact, He was not. Or, it may be that they were simply unfamiliar with the geography of Judea and asked directions to Bethlehem because they may have known He had been born there.

We cannot leave this matter of the star without mentioning that after it appeared to the magi in Persia, it then seems to have disappeared. They did not follow it to Jerusalem. But they did follow it to Bethlehem. What an amazing phenomenon! Matthew says that when the magi departed from Jerusalem for Bethlehem, "lo, the star (light) which they saw in the east, went before them, till it came and stood over where the young child was" (Matthew 2:9). How could a burning, fiery star in the heavens do this? Have you ever looked at the stars in the heavens and determined when one was directly overhead? It can't be done. A star that appears to be overhead to a person on the equator may also appear to be overhead to someone in Miami. The same light that led Israel through the wilderness led the magi to Bethlehem. It stood over the exact house where Joseph, Mary and the child Jesus lived. A star in the heavens could never do this.

The Magi had God's light to guide them. They also had something else to help them. God spoke to them in dreams. The Bible says He did. Matthew says, "And being warned of God in a dream" (Matthew 2:12). They knew it was God speaking to them and it was probably not the first time. Between dreams and a sign, the magi were compelled to make the long journey from their eastern homeland to Judea where they should have been living. "We are come", they announced, "to worship Him" (Matthew 2:2).

It is commonly thought that the magi arrived in Bethlehem at night. This is probably because they were supposedly following a star that could be seen only at night. However, the sheckinah glory could appear anytime and be seen day or night. It appeared to Saul of Tarsus on the Damascus road at noon. They may have arrived at night, but they could just as easily have arrived in broad daylight. The way Matthew 2:11 is worded, it sounds like everybody was up and awake, rather than the magi entering the house in the dark of the night.

The Gifts

When the magi from the east found the young child Jesus with Mary and Joseph, they fell down before the child and worshipped Him. They did not worship Mary and Joseph. They presented the child Jesus with gifts of gold, frankincense and myrrh. These gifts were given out of their "treasures", literally out of their chests, which indicates that the magi were wealthy men. They came with a whole luggage full of gifts. Since Joseph and Mary were not likely rich in worldly possessions, the gifts, primarily the gold, must have been a great help to them, especially when they went to Egypt. Their poverty is not exactly assumed. When they presented Jesus at the temple and offered a gift in his name and honor according to the law, they offered turtledoves. By law, if one could not afford more costly gifts, turtledoves were acceptable. It was the poorest of all the gifts. They gave what they could afford. God does not ask for more than that.

The gifts were not dime store trinkets, nor were they the kinds of gifts one would give to a child. These gifts were very special and appear to have spiritual significance. They were an indication that the magi were quite familiar with the Old Testament and might have known the meaning of the person of Christ. They must have been familiar with passages like Genesis 3:15; Numbers 24:17; Psalm 2:7-12,

Isaiah 7:14 and 9:6-7. The magi did not bring gifts for a child; they brought gifts for a King. They arrived in Jerusalem asking where they might find the child who was born King of the Jews. Furthermore, they must have understood that He, who would be Israel's King, would also be Israel's promised Prophet and Priest, One who would deliver Israel from her enemies and intercede before God for them. That explains the type of gifts given. If all this is so, it is strong evidence that the magi were not Persian Gentiles, nor were they astrologers, but were godly Jews who knew the Scriptures and believed them.

First, the gold. Gold is the metal of royalty, and therefore an appropriate gift for a king. They obviously believed that one day this child before them would govern the nation Israel and deliver them from their enemies. He would be their Savior King. Gold not only represented royalty but was also a basis for wealth. Wealth is the trademark of the Jewish people. God has blessed the Jews with the remarkable ability to amass wealth, even when they do not recognize God as the One who enables them to do it. Moses reminded Israel, saying, "And thou (Israel) say in thine heart, My power and the might of mine hand hath gotten me this wealth. But thou shalt remember the Lord thy God: for it is he that giveth thee power to get wealth, that he may establish his covenant which he sware unto thy fathers, as it is this day" (Deuteronomy 8:17-18). Genesis 13:2 says Abraham was very rich. It is hard to imagine a king wealthier than Solomon. When God gave Moses instructions

45

on the building of the tabernacle, He ordered the extensive use of gold throughout.

Gold is the first metal mentioned in Scripture and God proclaimed, "the gold of that land is good" (Genesis 2:11-12). When the magi presented the gift of gold to the child Jesus, they were acknowledging His kingship; therefore, their gift was prophetic; it said that the magi believed that this child would someday be their King.

Secondly, the frankincense. What is it? It is a gum resin that comes from a family of small trees and shrubs that grow in Arabia and along the east coast of Africa. The resin is obtained by tapping the trees or shrubs. The tapping is done by making a small cut about two inches long into the bark of the plant. An axe or specially designed tool is used to make this incision. A milky liquid exudes and hardens on exposure to air into droplets, or tears, which are then collected about two weeks later. The only processing done is the sorting and grading of the resin globules. This was usually done by the merchants who purchased the droplets from the collectors.

The globules are then used in perfumes, medicines and embalming. As a gift to the child Jesus, it may have implied that the magi recognized the priestly office of Jesus. Frankincense was one of the spices which was compounded with other spices into a perfume to be offered as incense to the Lord. It was so ordered by the Lord, and it was a serious sin to use an offering other than this particular incense offering. The mixture was used in meal offerings to the Lord but never used in a sin offering, (Leviticus 2:1-2, 5-11 and 15-16). It was also sprinkled on the twelve cakes of shewbread in the tabernacle that were eaten by Aaron and his sons. In this way frankincense was associated with worshipping the Lord. Because the priests intervened for the people of Israel before God, frankincense came to signify the offerings of prayers to the Lord. As incense was poured onto the altar of incense and smoke ascended upward, it represented the offering up of prayers, (Psalm 141:2). In Revelation we read, "golden vials full of odours (perfume), which are the prayers of the saints" (Revelation 5:8). The odors were a "sweet-smelling savour" (Ephesians 5:2). (cf. Revelation 8:3-4). The main ingredient of incense was frankincense and to the magi it might have spoken of the priestly ministry that would be undertaken by the child Jesus.

Thirdly, the myrrh. What is myrrh? Almost exactly like frankincense, it is a gum resin from a family of trees and shrubs that grow in the Arabian Peninsula and along the east coast of Africa. The aroma of myrrh is quite different from that of frankincense. As an aromatic gum, it is also used in making perfumes, medicines and used especially in embalming. It is first mentioned in Scripture in connection with oil used for anointing. It was mixed with other spices and olive oil and is called "an oil of holy ointment" (Exodus 30:25). Prophets, priests and kings were anointed because these men were chosen to their offices by the Lord. The use of the holy oil was restricted to these offices. The oil included myrrh.

When Christ came from heaven to earth, He came as the Messiah, the Anointed One, Israel's Christ.

The people of the Middle East used myrrh to embalm the deceased. This was especially common in Egypt, but it was common among the Jews also. "A mixture of myrrh and aloes" (John 19:39) was one of the burial spices used by Joseph of Arimathaea and Nicodemus when they wrapped the body of Jesus in linen clothes.

Did the magi know Jesus was born to die? In Acts we read that the church in Jerusalem who believed in Christ recognized that Jesus was the anointed Christ. It says, "For of a truth against thy holy child Jesus, whom thou hast anointed, both Herod, and Pontius Pilate, with the Gentiles, and the people of Israel, were gathered together" (Acts 4:27).

What shall we conclude about the gifts? The magi were godly Jews from somewhere in Mesopotamia who knew the Holy Scriptures. They were familiar with the promises of the Christ who was to come to Israel. Their gifts seem to say they believed He that was born King of the Jews was also the Prophet of whom Moses wrote, and the Priest who would offer up to God the perfect sacrifice for the sins of the world. The magi announced to all Jerusalem when they arrived, we "are come to worship him" (Matthew 2:2). They were led by a light to One who was and still is the Light of the world, the Lord Jesus Christ.

CHAPTER 4

Joseph and Mary

In Matthew's Gospel we read, "When as his mother Mary was espoused to Joseph" (Matthew 1:18). This opens up to us the question, what were the marriage customs in Bible times? What did it mean to be espoused?

The Greek word in Matthew 1:18 is a participle form of **mnesteuo** that can be translated 'having been.' It means having been promised in marriage. This was a binding covenant between two parties consisting usually of potential husband and wife and their families.

The participle is in the passive voice, implying that Joseph and Mary did not make the promise to each other directly, but the arrangement was made by other parties. Otherwise, the participle would have been in the active voice. It is quite likely that Mary's parents promised her to Joseph at either his request or that of his parents.

This particular Greek word, espoused, is used only three times in the New Testament; here, and in Luke 1:27 and 2:5. When the promise of marriage was agreed upon by both parties, a document was signed, though, there sometimes may have been exceptions to this formality.

It was customary for the two families and the prospective bride and groom to meet, with others present as witnesses. At the meeting, the groom would give a gift to the girl such as jewelry or some other

49

article of value. Sometimes only the signed document was offered, in which a man promised to marry a girl. He might repeat words to her like "see by this token thou art set apart for me, according to the Law of Moses and of Israel". This was not the actual marriage ceremony. That came later, often by as much as a year.

It was while Mary was promised to Joseph, but not yet married to him, that she conceived her child of the Holy Spirit of God. Why at this time? The Bible gives us the reason. The conception had to happen "before they came together" (Matthew 1:18). Otherwise, how would it be known that Joseph was not the father of the baby Jesus? Further evidence that Joseph was not the father was that Jesus was born while Mary was still a virgin. Naturally, we have only God's word for this, but God's word, being what it is, is enough.

When did the marriage take place? Matthew 1:24 implies that it was after the visit of the angel of the Lord to Joseph. The exact time probably cannot be determined, but it might be undogmatically assumed that nearly a full year had passed since the betrothal first began. The wedding took place very shortly after Mary conceived the baby Jesus. Nothing looked suspicious to the family or the public during the time before the marriage, if anyone cared to count backwards later. In Luke 2:5, "his espoused wife" may seem to imply that they were not yet married when they left for Bethlehem. A review of the grammar reveals that the participle used here is not aorist tense as it is in Matthew 1:18, but the perfect tense, implying that the espousal had been completed. It was over. They were now fully married. `Why bother with grammar research? Because tense in verbs is designed to answer the questions about when the action takes place and what kind of action it is. Of time and kind, the more important is kind of action. The chief function of a Greek tense is thus not to denote time, but progress.

The character of the action of the tense may be defined in three ways. 1.) Continuous action. 2.) Complete action. 3.) Occurring action. The use of the perfect tense in Luke 2:5 means the action has been completed, therefore, the Holy Spirit inspired Luke to use this tense that we might know that Joseph and Mary were married before they left Nazareth (lit. having been espoused, implying they no longer are espoused). The aorist tense is used in Matthew 1:18 when the action is continuous or indefinite. The families had agreed to the marriage of Joseph and Mary; the promise had been made; the contract had been signed; but the exact date of the marriage was indefinite.

In summary, Mary was promised to Joseph in an agreement between both families. If custom was followed, they were married in a marriage ceremony about one year later, though the ceremony is not actually mentioned. Very shortly before the marriage ceremony took place, Mary was informed by the Lord that she would become the mother of Israel's promised Messiah whom she conceived by the Holy

Spirit. Mary and Joseph refrained from a physical relationship until after the baby was born. At the very time or shortly after the wedding ceremony, a decree was issued by the Roman government that a census was to be taken and at which time individual taxes were to be paid. This gave Joseph and Mary a reason to leave Nazareth very soon after they were married, before anyone knew Mary was expecting this child, the secrecy of which, as we shall see, was of the highest importance.

Joseph and Mary's Dilemma

Joseph "being a just (righteous) man" (Matthew 1:19), means he obeyed the Mosaic Law. Joseph was the only man in Israel who was qualified to be the father of the Lord Jesus because of his genealogy. It is certain that Mary was a godly young woman because Luke wrote, "Fear not, Mary; for thou hast found favor with God" (Luke 1:30. The news to Mary that she was going to be the mother of the Lord was good news, but she must have wondered how Joseph would react. Never before in history had a virgin conceived a baby without a human father. How did Joseph react to Mary's announcement? It is certain she told Joseph alone, and perhaps later, Elisabeth.

Naturally, he was in disbelief. He knew he was not the father of this child, but then who would have been the father? Clearly, he did not believe Mary's explanation. He planned to end the espousal and upcoming marriage, but this posed several problems. First, a promise had been made and a contract signed.

Second, a dowry price had most likely been paid; how could that be returned? Third, he probably loved Mary very much and tried to think of a way to end the espousal without drawing public attention to it, an almost impossible thing to do. Fourth, what about his own reputation? Would anyone believe he was not the father? This would make him liable for the penalty imposed by the Mosaic Law. Fifth, the law was very severe concerning a woman becoming pregnant before she was married. What would people think of her? Matthew 1:20 says, "While he thought on these things." He must have turned the matter over in his mind repeatedly, day and night, trying to come up with a solution. What he did not yet know was he would never be able to resolve this matter to his own satisfaction. He could not come up with an answer, but we know now that he did not have to. God had the answer. Joseph would never have taken Mary as his wife except for one thing; God sent His angel to explain to Joseph that Mary was telling him the truth, the child was indeed conceived by the Holy Spirit. Joseph was instructed to take Mary as his wife. As he was a righteous and obedient man, Matthew says, "Joseph…did as the angel of the Lord had bidden him and took unto him his wife" (Matthew 1:24). In other words, they got married, probably right away. The marriage ceremony was carried out at the end of the espousal period, and nobody knew Mary was expecting this child when the wedding took place.

As for Mary, no one can know what soul searching she went through trying to compose a speech for

Joseph. When Joseph would ask her by whom she became pregnant, her explanation was, the Holy Spirit caused it. Who in their right mind would believe a story like that? Joseph did not believe it, and but for the intervention of the angel of the Lord, never would have accepted Mary's account.

Nobody would have believed Mary, so it was absolutely essential to keep the matter a secret. If they told anyone, Joseph would not have been able to put her away privily (secretly). Word travels fast. In order to keep Mary's pregnancy a secret, it was necessary for Joseph and Mary to leave Nazareth, but where could they go? God had the answer. His timing is absolutely perfect. All this comes about at the time the Roman government issued a decree "that all the world should be taxed" (Luke 2:1). Now Joseph and Mary had a reason to leave town. The short explanation is, since it was decreed that everyone should go to the place of his or her origin, where they were registered, they had to go to Bethlehem. Before anyone was aware of Mary's condition, the couple left for Bethlehem. It is implied in the words, in Luke's words, "And so it was, that, while they were there, the days were accomplished that she should be delivered" (Luke 2:6). They arrived there long before Mary was due to deliver the child. Who in Bethlehem knew or cared that Mary was expecting this child. The means of her pregnancy was a total secret.

Therefore, "When the fullness of time was come, God sent forth His Son, made of a woman, made under the law" (Galatians. 4:4). "The days were accomplished that she should be delivered, and she brought forth her firstborn Son" (Luke 2:6-7). The prophecy of Isaiah 7:14 was fulfilled which says in Matthew, "Behold a virgin shall be with child, and shall bring forth a son, and they shall call His name Emmanuel, which being interpreted is, God with us" (Matthew 1:23).

CHAPTER 5

The Virgin Birth

"Behold, a virgin shall be with child, and shall bring forth a son, and they shall call his name Emmanuel, which being interpreted is, God with us. Then Joseph being raised from sleep did as the angel of the Lord had bidden him, and took unto him his wife: and knew her not till she had brought forth her firstborn son: and he called his name Jesus." (Matthew 1:23-25).

One of the basic doctrines of the Christian faith is that of the supernatural conception and virgin birth of the Lord Jesus Christ. Heresy denies both. No one would ever have known such an event took place if it had not been recorded in the Scriptures. No one would have expected such a thing to take place for it never had happened before. Scripture was God-breathed into the minds of Matthew and Luke, who wrote exactly what God inspired them to write, neither adding to it, nor subtracting from it so much as a jot or tittle. When we open our Bibles, we have before us the details of Jesus conception and birth in English just as God gave it to Matthew and Luke in Greek. This naturally calls for trust in the Bible as being true. It is God's word on the matter and will remain so until somebody is able to prove that the accounts are falsified, inaccurate and not true.

God is the cause of accuracy in the Bible. He has been clear because He really wants the readers and hearers to know and understand His message. It is not difficult to find examples of God's carefulness and exactness in inspiring His word.

You have learned from a previous chapter that there are at least two towns named Bethlehem in Israel mentioned in the Bible. There was Bethlehem of Zebulun and Bethlehem of Ephraim. One is north of Jerusalem and the other is south. The northern Bethlehem is mentioned in Joshua 19:15. The southern Bethlehem is mentioned in Micah 5:2 and Matthew 2:5. Ephraim and Judea are names for the same place, so it says in Genesis 35:19. The prophets said Christ would be born in Bethlehem of Judea and the Lord wanted to make sure the right place was mentioned. The Jews were never confused about where Christ was to be born. They knew it was not Bethlehem of Zebulun because God made it clear by naming the place of Christ's birth as Bethlehem of Judea.

"And Enoch, the seventh from Adam" (Jude 1:14). Why was it necessary to mention that Enoch the prophet was the seventh generation from Adam? Is it not because there was a contemporary of Enoch's by the same name? The first Enoch was the son of Cain Genesis. 4:17, and he was the third generation from Adam. The second Enoch was the son of Jared and was the seventh generation from Adam. Cain's family had an evil heritage, but Jared's lineage can be traced back to Seth through whom there was a godly heritage. The Lord made it clear to Jude about which Enoch He was inspiring him to write. By the way, has anyone noticed that the New Testament writers fully trusted the accuracy of Old Testament history.

The effort to make the Scriptures clear and exact is a divine effort by the only One who has the power, ability and wisdom to produce absolute accuracy. We can say with David, "Thy word is very pure: therefore thy servant loveth it" (Psalm. 119:140). "My heart standeth in awe at thy word", Psalm. 119:161.

The virgin birth has been disputed, especially by unbelievers, because they reject the authority of the Scriptures. It has been attacked, perhaps, because critics thought it was the easiest doctrine to disprove. The resurrection was not so easy because there were so many witnesses who saw the risen Christ. Where were the witnesses to the supernatural conception? There was nobody. Where were the witnesses to the virgin birth? There were none except Joseph. There are not many references in the Bible to the virgin birth. Mark does not mention it and neither does John, though he does say that the Word became flesh, but he does not say how. Paul never mentions it but strongly implies he believed it. "For what the law could not do, in that it was weak through the flesh, God sending his own Son in the likeness of sinful flesh, and for sin, condemned sin in the flesh." (Roman 8:3). The twelve did not preach about it. It is exclusively the report in the New Testament of Matthew and Luke. How did Matthew and Luke know about the conception and virgin birth of Christ? The same way that Moses, who wrote Genesis, knew that God created the heavens and earth and Adam and

Eve; it was revealed to them by the Lord. Moses, Matthew and Luke wrote wholly by inspiration of God. The public did not know about the conception and virgin birth because they never heard about it and thought Joseph was Jesus' father. According to John 1:45 that's what the disciples also thought, until Matthew and Luke revealed otherwise.

Unbelieving philosophers, rationalists, historians, theologians, and scientists discount the virgin birth as a fact of history. Some say it was an impossibility, and it was. It could never have happened. However, it did. Others say it does not matter and they do not care if it happened; believing it, they say, it is not essential to our salvation. But, it does matter very much. "If we receive the witness of men, the witness of God is greater" (I John. 5:9; cf. I John. 4:2-3). If someone says Jesus could have been born the child of two earthly parents and still have been sinless, how then could He have been God in the flesh?

There is a serious danger in denying that Jesus was born of the virgin Mary. A denial rarely stands by itself. It will be accompanied by other denials of things the Bible teaches. To deny Christ's conception and virgin birth is to deny His deity and Messiahship. The Old Testament says a virgin would conceive and bear Israel's Messiah who would be Emmanuel, God with us (Isa. 7:14; 9:6). Denial of Christ's conception and virgin birth is rejection of prophecy on which we rely as one of the proofs of the veracity of the Scriptures. If the virgin birth is denied just because one chooses to not believe it, though there is

Scriptural evidence for it, then every other doctrine can be denied for the same reason. Though the virgin birth does not have the support of public witnesses unlike the miracles the Lord Jesus performed, and His resurrection, it does have strong credentials.

First, The Bible SAYS Jesus was virgin born. If this statement is not true, how can it be proven it isn't? Second, the Scriptures present the virgin birth as true, but if it is not, how can we know any other statements in the Bible are true? The integrity of the Scriptures is at stake here.

Third, not only is the virgin birth challenged, but the supernatural conception is challenged as well. The conception implies that there was a departure from the natural laws of procreation. It further implies that the element of the supernatural is involved in the person of Christ. The Bible clearly states that Mary's conception took place as a result of the intervention of the Holy Spirit of God without the involvement of the human element. The implication begins in Genesis 3:15 and the concept is followed throughout the Scriptures. The Seed of the woman was without the contribution of a human father. There was no part of Christ that had it's source in Mary or Joseph; not His Spirit, not His body, not His blood, nor His personality. Does Galatians 4:4 contradict this? It says He was "made of a woman". The Greek word for "made" has a wide range of meanings, including born or became. The word occurs twice in this verse. Christ was born of a woman, born under the law. He entered the human race the way all mankind does. He was born into it. The Word became flesh without the presence of a human gene pool. A gene pool was not needed. In the many genealogies given in the Bible we read that man begat or was the father of so and so, but a mother is rarely mentioned. In Genesis 3:15 this order is reversed. In 1 Corinthians 15:45-47 the second Adam, who was Christ, was made a quickening or living Spirit and was the Lord from heaven. Neither Adam nor the Lord from heaven had a human father. John 1:1-3 calls the Lord Jesus the Word of God, saying He was God in the beginning. Verse 14 says that the Word became flesh and dwelt with men. Isaiah 7:14 prophesies that a virgin shall conceive and we thus have in one and the same verse statements concerning both the conception and the virgin birth of Christ. They must be considered together. Matthew 1:22-23 supports this idea, as does Isaiah 7:14. Both prophecy and inspiration of the Scriptures play a role in this doctrine.

The virgin birth is not mentioned very often in the Scriptures. Only Matthew and Luke give an account of it. In fact, Luke does not even directly say Christ was born of the virgin Mary, but says her conception took place while she was still a virgin (Luke 1:27, 31; 34-35). When Mary says, I know not a man, that does not necessarily mean she would continue in that state before Jesus was born or after she was married, yet that was the way it had to be for Christ to be virgin born. Matthew 1:18 says the promise of a supernatural conception was fulfilled and verses 23-25 are the only verses that say without obscurity that when Christ was born, Mary was still a virgin.

If the doctrine of the virgin birth is so important, why is it that it was not preached during Christ's earthly ministry? Why did the twelve not preach about it, and why is the subject not addressed in the four gospels after Christ was born? Some undogmatic reasons may be suggested for this nearly one hundred percent silence. First, it was not known by more than a few people, namely Mary and Joseph, and perhaps Elisabeth and Zacharias with whom Mary may have shared the information, (Luke 1:45). They would have believed Mary but would not have shared this news with anyone else. To do so would have brought scandal and embarrassment upon the whole family. The reason for this silence is simple. Nobody would have believed it. Second, a virgin conception and birth could not be neither proven nor disproven. There were no witnesses to verify anything. The shepherds did not know the baby they saw lying in a manger was virgin born for the angels had not disclosed this fact. Simeon and Anna, who saw this newly born baby, did not know it. The twelve apostles did not know it until it was revealed to them, either by the Lord after His resurrection during His forty-day ministry on earth when He opened their eyes concerning Himself as revealed in the Old Testament (Luke 24:44-45), or they learned it from Matthew and Luke. They certainly did not learn it from Mary, for the Bible says she "kept all these things, and pondered them in her heart" (Luke 2:19).

Ponder means to weigh and thoughtfully consider them in the mind. This is not the same thing as sharing news with others. It is certain Joseph told no one. He was going to put Mary away "privily" or secretly. How could he have accomplished this if he had been telling people about Mary? The twelve apostles were sent forth as witnesses, meaning they preached on the things they heard and saw (Acts 4:20). As far as the record shows, they did not even personally know the Lord before He was thirty years of age nor did they know anything about his childhood years or youth. Since they were not witnesses of His conception and birth or upbringing, they did not include these matters in their preaching. It was Mary's and Joseph's secret. It is most likely that she did not tell Jesus' brothers and sisters. They did not believe in Him. This does not mean they hated Him, only that they did not believe His claims. It seems they might have considered Jesus to be a bit eccentric. How could they have remained in unbelief if they had known Jesus was conceived and born of a virgin? Most likely they learned about it after it was revealed by inspiration for publication by Matthew and Luke. Matthew and Luke had an Old Testament verse to prove the truth of their statements.

Of all the accusations against the Lord, slander about His birth was not one of them. If they had known Joseph was not His father, it would have been such a strong point against Him. His birth was always considered legitimate and Joseph was always thought of as Jesus' father. It was never questioned by the public. Knowledge of the virgin birth would have changed all this.

Why did Paul not mention the conception and virgin birth in his epistles? He must have known about it. Luke, who wrote about it, was one of Paul's traveling companions and the historian of Paul's apostolic evangelistic missionary journeys. Paul wrote to the Corinthian church, "Wherefore henceforth know we no man after the flesh: yea, though we have known Christ after the flesh, yet now henceforth know we him no more" (II Corinthians 5:16). Paul wrote only by inspiration and mentions the deity of Christ, His pre-existence and His sinlessness, all related to Christ being supernaturally conceived and virgin born.

And so, "when the fullness of time was come, God sent forth His Son, made of a woman, made under the law" (Galatians 4:4). "The days were accomplished that she should be delivered, and she brought forth her firstborn Son" (Luke 2:6-7). The prophecy of Isaiah made over seven hundred years earlier was fulfilled which says, "Behold, a virgin shall be with child, and shall bring forth a son, and they shall call his name Emmanuel, which being interpreted is, God with us" (Matthew 1:23). The virgin birth should be considered a fact of history because it is recorded in the book of accurate historical knowledge.

The conclusion, therefore, is that Christ was conceived of the Holy Spirit and born of the virgin Mary; that the conception was supernatural and miraculous; that the virgin birth forms a basis for the doctrine of the deity of Christ; that it explains His sinless perfection; and that it fulfills the prophecies of the Old Testament, which is a chief proof of the veracity of the Scriptures. "Hereby know ye the Spirit of God: Every spirit that confesseth that Jesus Christ is come in the flesh is of God: And every spirit that confesseth not that Jesus Christ is come in the flesh is not of God: and this is the spirit of antichrist, whereof ye have heard that it should come; and even now already is in the world" (I John 4:2-3).

The Genealogies of Joseph and Mary

Matthew and Luke record genealogies related to Christ. When they are compared, they do not read alike. The genealogies are not the same. This has provided critics who discredit the authenticity of the Scriptures with supposed cannon fodder to blast away at the Bible's credibility and accuracy.

An understanding of the two genealogies will help the reader to appreciate the thoroughness with which God has inspired His Word to report facts and truths.

Genealogies were necessary for Israel for three reasons. First, to keep a record that would verify who the priests were. Second, to verify who had the right to be the king of Israel. Only one man in Israel at any given time had this right. Third, to keep a record of which of the twelve tribes each Israelite belonged to. (II Chronicles 31:16-19; Ezra 2:62). The genealogy in the first chapter of Matthew is that of the kings of Israel; first, as a united nation, and later, restricted to the southern Kingdom of Judah when Israel was divided into two kingdoms. The claim that Jesus was born king of the Jews could have been verified by the genealogical records. Did anyone bother to check and see? The outline of the first 16 verses of Matthew is as follows.

I. The genealogy of Jesus Christ. Matthew 1:1.

II. The father of Israel, Abraham, Matthew 1:1.

III. The line to the royal family, Matthew 1:2.

IV. Judas, (Judah) the father of the royal family, Matthew 1:2-6.

V. The kings of united Israel, Matthew 1:6-7.

VI. The kings of the divided kingdoms. The kings of the northern kingdom of Israel are excluded and only the kings of the tribe of Judah, the southern kingdom, are listed. Matthew 1:7-11.

VII. The men who would have been kings, but there was no longer a kingdom, Matthew 1:12-16, I Chronicles 9:1.

VIII. Jesus Christ, the last king of the reunited kingdom, Matthew 1:16. This will not come to pass until the millennial kingdom is established which is yet future after the Tribulation.

Joseph, the supposed father of Jesus, would have been the king of Israel instead of a carpenter in Nazareth had there been a kingdom to govern. We wonder how many people in Israel knew that? The office of king was that of an absolute monarchy. The right to rule passed from father to son. Being the eldest son of Joseph, the Lord Jesus Christ had the right to rule over Israel. Even though Joseph had no biological relationship to Jesus, he raised Jesus as his son. The public did not even think of Jesus as Joseph's adopted son. They thought Joseph was Jesus' biological father. Looking over the genealogy in Matthew, the first thing established is nationality. The kings of Israel must be Israelites, descendants of Abraham. The second thing is that they must come from Jacob's son, Judas (Judah), the father of the royal family. The third fact established is that the kings must be able to trace their lineage back to David, the first king over Israel from the line of Judah. When the kingdom was divided into two, during the reign of Rehoboam, the genealogy was traced through the kings of the southern kingdom of Judah rather than the kings of the northern kingdom of Israel. None of the kings of Israel qualified to be king.

Why was the kingdom divided in the days of king Rehoboam, who succeeded his father Solomon? God divided the kingdom, a result of Solomon's twenty years of apostasy, as a means of punishment. A pretender to the throne named Jeroboam rivaled

Rehoboam for supremacy over Israel which resulted in a long drawn-out war between Israel and Judah.

Matthew is an ascending genealogy of the kings of Judah. The kings of the northern kingdom of Israel are not included. It shows that the Lord Jesus Christ had a right to rule as King over all the nation of Israel. The men who were the only ones who had a legal right to govern Israel had to be Israelites, of the lineage of Judah and of the family of David. Jesus had all three of the qualifications.

The apostle Paul had this to say in Titus about genealogies, "But avoid foolish questions, and genealogies, and contentions, and strivings about the law; for they are unprofitable and vain" (Titus 3:9). In Paul's letter to Timothy, he says, "Neither give heed to fables and endless genealogies, which minister questions, rather than godly edifying, which is in faith: so do" (1 Timothy 1:4). If genealogies are so important, why are we told to avoid them? We must rightly divide the nation of Israel from the church called the Body of Christ. They are two completely different entities. Genealogies were important to Israel for reasons stated above, (1 Chronicles 9:1). The church does not have a priesthood nor does it have kings. The Lord Jesus Christ is never referred to as the King of the church. He is called the Head of the church, (Ephesians 1:22). The church is not called a nation made of tribes or families so genealogies are not needed for any reason. They mean nothing to the church. To try to make them mean something would only cause problems.

We are left to wonder how many Jews in Israel could trace their genealogy all the way back to one of Jacob's twelve sons as well as the Lord Jesus could. Mary and Joseph knew they were descendants of King David; they knew they belonged to the royal family of Israel.

The genealogy in the Gospel of Luke is quite different from Matthew's. Luke's is not a genealogy of kings. While Matthew's genealogy follows the ascending line of rulers of Israel and Judah, starting with Abraham, Luke's descending line starts with Jesus and goes back to the very beginning of humanity, namely Adam. While Matthew presents Jesus as the King of Israel, Luke presents Jesus as the Son of man. Therefore, we find in Luke's Gospel emphasis on His humanity rather than His royalty.

A widely accepted explanation for two different lines of ancestry is that Matthew gave Joseph's line of descent and Luke gave Mary's line of descent. Both Joseph and Mary could trace their lineage back to David. This seems a reasonable explanation. If Heli was Mary's father, he would have been Joseph's father-in-law. The words *"the Son"* (Luke 3:23) are not in the Greek text. It was placed there by the King James translator assigned this passage who thought this would make the passage clearer. It did not. In Greek, the verse reads, "which was of Heli". Several commentators have noted that the words in parenthesis in Verse 23 (as was supposed) are a questionable translation of the Greek. The Greek word is **enomizeto** and comes from the root word *nomos*, which means law, in reference to the establishment of legal custom. Joseph was related to Heli according to the legal customs of his day. This would make sense if Heli was the father-in-law and not the father of Joseph. Matthew Henry[1] says the expression "as was supposed" in Luke 3 should be translated "as was entered into the books" (Luke 3:23). He meant that the records would show that Jesus was a descendant of David by Mary as well as by Joseph. How many men in Israel could make that claim in Jesus' day? The genealogy shows that God made Jesus doubly accredited as the rightful heir to David's throne. If anyone in Jesus' day refused to accept Matthew and Luke's report, they need only check the records that were kept and carefully guarded which would show Jesus' ancestry. It was there in black and white, two lists to check, and one would have been sufficient.

Jesus was not only from Adam in the sense of His genealogy, but also in another way. God created Adam's body directly from the dust of the ground, but God created Christ's body as well. Neither Joseph nor Mary contributed one gene or drop of blood to the body of Jesus.

Where are the genealogical records today? They apparently are missing. It might be that they disappeared when the second temple was destroyed. Unless they are discovered at some point in the future, the only records that can be appealed for the

---

[1] Henry, Matthew, Matthew Henry's Commentaries, Vol. V, p. 618, Fleming H. Revell Company, New York, New York

conception and birth of Jesus to are those of the New Testament, namely the Gospels of Luke and Matthew.

The Problem With Jechonias

In the genealogy in Matthew 1:11-12 there is mention of a man named Jechonias. It should first be noted that he is known by other names in the Bible. In 1 Chronicles 3:16-17 he is called Jeconiah. In 2 Kings 24:12-15 he is called Jehoiachin. In addition, in Jeremiah 22:24 he is known as Coniah. Jechonias is the Greek spelling of these three Hebrew names.

Who was he? He was the king of the southern kingdom of Judah at the time of Nebuchadnezzar's invasion of the land of the Jews. More importantly, he was the king through whom the unbroken line of descent was to pass in the genealogy of Christ back to king David. That is why his name appears in the lineage of Jesus through Joseph in Matthew 1:11-12.

There is a problem which affects his place in the line of descent. The Lord ordered Jeremiah to denounce Jechonias, and the Holy Spirit inspired him to record it. Jeremiah wrote, "Write ye this man childless, a man that shall not prosper in his days: for no man of his seed shall prosper, sitting upon the throne of David, and ruling any more in Judah" (Jeremiah 22:30).

If Jechonias was childless, how could the absolute Monarchy continue? With the line broken, how could there be a direct connection between Christ and David? Before it is concluded that the curse was irrevocable, consideration should be given to a solution that would reinstate him. The first part of the denunciation was that Jechonias would remain childless and could never bear a son who would be heir to the throne. It appears that this denunciation was lifted because 1 Chronicles 3:17-18 lists eight children by name who were the sons of Jechonias. When Nebuchadnezzar captured Jerusalem, Jechonias surrendered and was taken captive, with his mother, and was carried to Babylon as a prisoner of war.

The second denunciation was that he would never prosper as long as he lived. It seemed that this would be the case since he was in prison in Babylon, and he was about eighteen years old at that time. 2 Kings 25:27 says he was in prison for thirty-seven years. King Nebuchadnezzar died sometime during this imprisonment and a new king named Evil Meradoch released Jechonias from prison. The next verse says the new king dealt kindly with him. He set the throne of Jechonias above the throne of other imprisoned rulers. He was given civilian clothing to replace prison garb. He was given a cash allowance and ate at the king's table. We are lead to conclude that Jechonias did prosper because the denunciation was reversed.

The third denunciation was that none of the offspring of Jechonias would occupy David's throne. This would have been true if he had not fathered children, but he had eight sons. If the first two denunciations were reversed, why could not the third also? So, was it? If the third denunciation was not reversed, then the Messiah could not descend to David through Jechonias and Solomon. It is believed that while Jechonias was in prison, he repented and asked the Lord to forgive him. He named his son Salathiel, which means, "I asked of God". He prayed about matters. God indicated His forgiveness by giving Jechonias children. When the Jews were released after seventy years of captivity in Babylon, one of the leaders of the return to Judah was Jechonias' grandson Zorobabel (Zerubbabel). He led the first of three groups of Jews in their return to Judah. He was a leader in the rebuilding of the temple, and he helped reorganize the priesthood. He helped to get all the returnees registered according to their genealogies. In addition, he helped to restore the observance of the Passover.

The exiled Jews obviously did not think of Zorobabel as still under the curse of the denunciation. He appears to have been a godly man and a spiritual leader. This may well be due to his upbringing by a grandfather who had turned his heart to the Lord. The postexilic prophets such as Zechariah speak highly of Zorobabel (Zechariah 4:7-10).

Even as the king of Babylon had pardoned Jechonias and released him from prison, it appears that God in His grace and mercy had forgiven him also and reinstated him in the Messianic lineage. This assures that the Lord Jesus Christ would be able to make His rightful claim to the Davidic throne through the genealogy of Joseph and the lineage of the kings of Judah.

CHAPTER 6

The Incarnation

Which of the fundamental beliefs of Christianity has not been attacked, doubted and denied, not only by atheists, agnostics, and skeptics, but also by religious scholars?

When Jesus was born, He was referred to as Emmanuel which means "God with us" (Matthew 1:23; Isaiah. 7:14). These are the only two verses in the Bible where this is found. They shall call His name Emmanuel, but who were "they"? Was it Joseph and Mary? Did they call His name Emmanuel? Was it the Jews? Was it the prophets? Since Jesus was wholly "God with us", who was it that knew this profound truth better than God Himself? The triune Godhead called Jesus "God with us". During the millennium, Israel will call Him Emmanuel. He did not cease to be with the Godhead just because He became flesh and was with man. This title was given to Him, thus fulfilling Scripture. The Scriptures are God's word. The Lord spoke by the prophet Isaiah and indicated what Jesus' title was to be, namely, Emmanuel. Isaiah reads, "Therefore the Lord Himself shall give you a sign; Behold, a virgin shall conceive, and bear a son, and shall call (the Lord...shall call) his name Immanuel"(Isaiah 7:14). Isaiah does not give us enough information to lead us to conclude the virgin birth refers to Mary. How many virgin women conceived when they had their first relationship with a man? It takes the fulfillment of

74

prophecy in Matthew chapter one to explain Isaiah 7:14. We could not be certain Isaiah's prophecy was a reference to Mary without the angel's explanation in Matthew 1:23.

Paul says, "For in him dwelleth all the fullness of the Godhead bodily" (Colossians 2:9). Paul warns the Colossian assembly to beware of the things that would destroy their belief and understanding of who Christ is. The philosophies, traditions and deceitful teachings could lead some away from the person of Christ. They would not grasp the meaning of Emmanuel, God with us, in bodily form. Those who reject the incarnation do not believe the fullness that could dwell in a newborn baby. "For it pleased *the Father* that in him should all fullness dwell" (Colossians 1:19). That was the plan from before the earth was created. Christ is the visible image of the invisible God.

What was the purpose for the incarnation? At least fourteen Scriptural reasons can be given. First, to reveal the Father. John says "No man hath seen God at any time; the only begotten Son, which is in the bosom of the Father, He hath declared *him* (John 1:18). "Philip saith unto him, Lord, shew us the Father, and it sufficeth us. Jesus saith unto him, Have I been so long time with you, and yet hast thou not known me, Philip? He that hath seen me hath seen the Father; and how sayest thou *then*, shew us the Father?" (John 14:8-9). Those who saw Jesus saw the Father as much as they will ever see Him. This is a bold, daring claim to deity. There is a remarkable likeness between the Father and the Son. Hebrews 1:1-3 says Jesus is the express image of the Father. In the Old Testament, God the Father made Himself known through names like Elohim, Jehovah, Adonai, El Shaddai and others. Let us not forget the use of plural pronouns that refer to the Godhead like "us", "we" and "our". "Let us make man in our image" (Genesis 1:26). In the New Testament, God the Father is made known by His Son. How wonderful it must have been to have known the Father who could be experienced. His love and tenderness, His law and discipline, a Father who would give to retrieve a lost humanity.

The second reason for the incarnation was to destroy the works of the devil. John says, "He that committeth sin is of the devil; for the devil sinneth from the beginning. For this purpose the Son of God was manifested, that he might destroy the works of the devil" (I John 3:8). The works of the devil are so terrible. He is a murderer who destroys life; a liar who destroys truth, and a betrayer who destroys trust. As a murderer, he influences people to kill other people, especially godly people. He influenced Cain to kill his righteous brother Abel, (I John 3:12). When the devil's influence is coupled with man's sinful nature, that is a deadly combination.

As a liar, the devil extinguishes light. Without light, people live in darkness. The apostle Paul says, "In whom the god of this world (Satan) hath blinded the minds of them which believe not, lest the light of the glorious gospel of Christ, who is the image of God, should shine unto them" (2 Corinthians 4:4). The only hope of man's deliverance from spiritual darkness is in hearing the gospel of Christ, (2 Corinthians. 4:5-6 and 13). As a betrayer, the devil can never be trusted. However, he's hard to pick out of the crowd sometimes. Why is that? He masquerades as an angel of light. He was the influence that pushed Judas over the edge to betray Christ. Judas was one of the twelve disciples and not one of the other eleven could have guessed that Judas would commit such an awful betrayal. "Then entered Satan into Judas surnamed Iscariot, being of the number of the twelve" (Luke 22:3). How clever the devil is to hide his workers among the saints. Judas did the same things, said the same things as the other disciples, and heard the teachings of Jesus. What a shock to the disciples when they learned that Judas betrayed Jesus into the hands of His enemies.

The third reason for the incarnation was to establish the kingdom of Israel from which all nations will benefit. God has always had a plan to divide man's history into ages. Satan inserted himself into man's history to destroy God's plans and establish his own program. He wants to be worshiped like the Lord, Jesus Christ. The conflict that resulted has caused people to choose whom they will serve. Joshua states an interdispensational principle. "And if it seem evil unto you to serve the LORD, choose you this day whom ye will serve; whether the gods which your fathers served that *were* on the other side of the flood (river), or the gods of the Amorites, in whose land ye dwell: but as for me and my house, we will serve the Lord" (Joshua 24:15). Satan is the ruler of the gods of this world. To serve those gods is to serve the devil. Christ will return to this world from heaven and insert Himself into the history of the human race, depose the religions of the god of this world system and reign as King of kings and Lord of lords.

The fourth reason for the incarnation was to put away sin and save sinners. Paul tells Timothy, "This is a faithful saying, and worthy of all acceptation, that Christ Jesus came into the world to save sinners; of whom I am chief" (I Timothy 1:15). John says "And ye know that he was manifested to take away our sins; and in him is no sin" (I John 3:5). Christ came to take away the sum total of all our transgressions, a number no man can count. Our own personal sins are in that number. Sin means missing the mark, either deliberately or in ignorance. Either way, we have missed the mark of God's will, purpose and righteousness. The Lord Jesus did not atone for our sins. To atone means to cover, to hide from view. He did something far better. He took away our sin. All of our sin is gone forever, never to be remembered or recalled. It seems that today people are unconcerned about their sins. They deny them or excuse them. Some are in agony over their burden of sin and loathe it, hating every evil deed. For those, we have good news, a permanent solution for their sin problem, a balm for their soul. Christ was manifested to take away all their sin, forever. The penalty of sin is removed. In place of the wages of sin, is life;

everlasting, never-ending life, and the promise of spending eternity with Christ. Who is this Christ who takes away our sin? He is the Lord Jesus Christ, the Son of God. He is the Word become flesh, the incarnate, virgin born Son of God. He is the Lamb of God who takes away the sin of the world and offers the gift of everlasting life to whosoever will believe in and receive Christ as their Savior. He offers the gift of life which needs only to be appropriated. In Him was no sin, ever. He never missed the mark.

A fifth reason for the incarnation was to reveal the truth. "Pilate therefore said unto him, art thou the king then? Jesus answered, thou sayest that I am a king. To this end was I born, and for this cause came I into the world, that I should bear witness unto the truth. Everyone that is of the truth heareth my voice" (John 18:37). The world is filled with the devil's lies. It is popular today to think there is no such thing as absolute truth. If it is truth man has invented or imagined, that might be true. If it is truth revealed by the Lord, it must be absolute and at the same time, dispensationaly understood. All the truth we need to know about spiritual matters has been made known to us in the Scriptures. Matters about the historical past, the present times and the prophetic future are in the Scriptures. God has reported accurate history and it can be completely trusted. God tells the truth about everything we need to know.

A sixth reason for the incarnation was so that Jesus could die. Without becoming like man, without having a human body, He could not die. It seems from the Scriptures that spirit beings do not die. Angels do not die. The Lord Jesus, in order to die, had to have a body that would die. "But we see Jesus, who was made a little lower than the angels for the suffering of death, crowned with glory and honor; that he by the grace of God should taste death for every man" (Hebrews 2:9). "But made himself of no reputation, and took upon him the form of a servant, and was made in the likeness of men: And being found in fashion as a man, he humbled himself, and became obedient unto death, even the death of the cross" (Philippians 2:7-8).

Many religious entities think that belief in the incarnation is not necessary for salvation. Apparently they have not read the verse in 1 John which says "Hereby know ye the Spirit of God: Every spirit that confesseth that Jesus Christ is come in the flesh is of God: And every spirit that confesseth not that Jesus Christ is come in the flesh is not of God: and this is the spirit of antichrist, whereof ye have heard that it should come; and even now already is it in the world" (1 John 4:2-3). The nation of Israel was under the law and the church called the body of Christ is under grace, and both Israel and the church are required to believe in the incarnation.

A seventh reason for Christ being born into the human family is stated by Paul, 'to redeem them that were under the law" (Galatians 4:5). Who was under the Mosaic Law? The law was given to Israel. The Jews were subject to it until, 1) God cast Israel aside, (Romans 11:15). 2) Until God afflicted the nation with spiritual blindness and deafness, (Romans 11:8). 3) Until 70 AD when the temple with the Holy of Holies, where God met His people, was destroyed and there was no place for the priesthood to function on behalf of the people. Paul announced to the Jews in the synagogues of Galatia, "But if ye be led of the Spirit, ye are not under the law" (Galatians 5:18). When he wrote his epistle to the church in Rome, he said, "For sin shall not have dominion over you: for ye are not under the law, but under grace" (Romans 6:14). Neither the Jews nor the Gentiles were under the law because they were redeemed from the curse of the law.

An eighth reason for Christ's being born was to make believers adoptive sons of God, (Galatians 4:5). Every regenerated Christian is a member of the family of God. We, both men and women, are the adoptive children of God and He is our heavenly Father.

A ninth reason why Christ was born into this world was to make every believer an "heir of God through Christ" (Galatians 4:7). Has anybody ever turned down an inheritance? Perhaps, for some strange reason, they have, but it must be a rare occurrence. God has an inheritance planned for us and no one will reject God's offer. To use the vernacular, it's already a done deal. "But when the fullness of time was come, God sent forth his Son, made of a woman, made under the law, To redeem them that were under the law, that we might receive the adoptions of sons. And because ye are sons, God hath sent forth the Spirit of his Son into your hearts, crying, Abba, Father. Wherefore thou are no more a servant, but a son: and if a son, then an heir of God through Christ" (Galatians 4:4-7). All of this because God sent forth His Son.

A tenth reason is given in Mark 2:17. The Lord said He came into the world "not to call the righteous, but sinners to repentance. A person who enjoys perfect health does not need a physician. But one who is sick needs a doctor. By the same token, a righteous person does not need to be saved, but it is the exact opposite for a sinner. The problem is, as stated in the scriptures, "there is none righteous, no, not one" (Romans 3:10). Romans 3:23 says "all have sinned and come short of the glory of God." The Lord came to call sinners to repent and believe in Him as the Savior of lost sinners.

An eleventh reason given for Christ's coming into the world is given in Mark 10:45. He came into the world "to give his life a ransom for many". What is a ransom? It is paying a price for the release of a person from bondage or captivity. The human race is in bondage to sin. No one can set their self free from sin. A person who has the ability and capacity to pay a ransom is needed. Is anyone more able than the Lord Jesus Christ to pay the required price? The wages of sin is death and the Lord Jesus Christ paid the wages of sin for every sinner. We are bought with a price, namely, the shed blood of a dying Savior who has cleansed every repenting sinner from all sin.

A twelfth reason for Christ being born into this world was to do His Father's will. "Jesus said unto them, My meat is to do the will of him that sent me, and to finish his work" (John 4:34).

A thirteenth reason which the Lord accomplished by being born into this world was that those who believed in Him might enjoy abundance of life. "The thief cometh not, but for to steal, and to kill, and to destroy: <u>I am come that they (the lost sheep of Israel) might have life, and that they might have it more abundantly</u>" (John 10:10).

A fourteenth reason for Christ coming into the world is yet future. He came into the world to be Israel's King. "Pilate therefore said unto him, Art thou a king then? Jesus answered, Thou sayest that I am a king. To this end was I born, and for this cause came I into the world, that I should bear witness unto the truth" (John 18:37). At the Second Coming, the Lord Jesus Christ will establish Israel's kingdom and take His rightful place on David's throne and rule Israel and the world as King of all kings.

Many of these reasons, if not all, are braided together and work in union and wisdom to fulfill the great eternal purpose of the triune Godhead in sending Christ Jesus into the world to save lost mankind.

CHAPTER 7

The Fugitives

Where did Joseph and Mary go after the rites of Mary's purification? Did they return to Bethlehem, or did they return to Nazareth? The question has arisen because of the statement in Luke which says, "And when they had performed all things according to the law of the Lord, they returned into Galilee, to their own city Nazareth" (Luke 2:39). Did Joseph and Mary return to Galilee as soon as they had fulfilled the requirements of the Mosaic Law in the temple in Jerusalem, or did they return to the little town of Bethlehem? In the case of childbirth, the law ordered thirty-three or sixty-six days to complete the rite of purification, which Mary was obligated to obey.

Joseph and Mary lived in Nazareth when they were first married. When Joseph learned that Mary was expecting her first child, and before the public was aware of this, they left for Bethlehem. The Roman government decreed that a census be taken and that everybody had to be registered in the place of their origin. This gave Joseph and Mary a reason to leave Nazareth, no other explanation to family and friends being necessary. They went to Bethlehem and while they were living there, the time came for Mary to be delivered. After Jesus was born, they spent the next thirty three to sixty six days fulfilling the requirements of the law of purification.

Nearly two years after Christ was born, "wise men from the east" arrived in Jerusalem to pay homage to "he that is born king of the Jews" (Matthew 2:1-2). They did not know where Jesus was but most likely thought He would have been in Jerusalem. When Herod learned of the arrival of the wise men and was informed as to their inquiry, he called for the chief priests and scribes who told him the Messiah would be born in Bethlehem of Judea. Herod sent the wise men to Bethlehem to search for the child with orders to return and tell him what they found. Did the wise men go to Bethlehem or Nazareth to search for the child? They never went back to Jerusalem as requested, but they did find the young child who was nearly two years old by that time.

It has been suggested that the star they saw in the east, and which appeared to guide them to the place where the young child was, would not have been needed if they went to Bethlehem. However, if the child was in Nazareth, then they were given wrong directions and needed the star to guide them to the right place. Bethlehem is only about five miles from Jerusalem, but Nazareth is about seventy miles distant and the star would have been a great help in guiding them to the right place, if Nazareth in Galilee had been the right place. They were warned by an angel not to return to Jerusalem to tell Herod of the whereabouts of the child.

Herod waited anxiously for a report from the wise men but none ever came. When he realized after a time that they would not be returning, he was enraged and "sent forth, and slew all the children that were in Bethlehem, and in all the coasts thereof, from two years old and under" (Matthew 2:16), causing great grief and mourning. The Satanic attempt to kill the child Jesus did not work because Joseph and Mary were not in Bethlehem. Were they in Nazareth? They were not in Nazareth; they had fled to Egypt. Did they somehow learn of Herod's terrible plan to kill the child? They did, but not from any man. God sent an angel to inform Joseph of Herod's intentions and ordered him to take his wife and the child Jesus and flee to Egypt and remain there until He told him it was safe to return home. Joseph did as instructed and fled in the dark of the night to avoid being detected. This explains why Jesus was not killed with the other children in and around Bethlehem. They stayed in Egypt until Herod died at which time God's angel appeared to tell Joseph it was safe to return to Israel. The question remains; did they go to Egypt from Bethlehem or Nazareth?

Luke does not mention the journey to Egypt or the visit of the wise men from the east. Matthew does not mention the Shepherds seeing the new born child in Bethlehem nor the slaughter of the innocent children. The accounts in Matthew and Luke do not contradict each other, they give supplementary information.

When the information in the two Gospels of Matthew and Luke is dovetailed, it seems most likely that the following occurred. First, Joseph and Mary lived in Bethlehem after the days of Mary's purification. Acquiring a house indicates they had not planned to return to Nazareth any time soon. It was important for plenty of time to elapse before returning to Nazareth to ensure that people would not be curious about when Christ was born. A belated return would keep them from asking questions. The Jews would never have accepted the story of the conception and virgin birth so this had to be kept a secret for the time being. In Bethlehem they had a house in which to live, indicating they intended to stay there awhile. Joseph was a carpenter and could easily have built a house on land belonging to his family. Until the house was finished, they lived in a small inn, and conceivably, it was the only inn in a village as small as Bethlehem. It was during the stay at the inn that Mary gave birth to the Lord Jesus.

On the other side of the coin, it might be argued that they had a house in Nazareth and it could have been the house referred to in Matthew 2:11, the house where the wise men saw the young boy Jesus. The wise men were guided there by a star. Why was a star, the Sheikinah light, needed to guide the wise men five miles to Bethlehem? They already knew in which town to look for the child. In fact, the light was not needed to lead the men to Bethlehem or anywhere else. It was needed to pinpoint the exact house where the family was to be found. Since several babies were killed by Herod, we can reasonably assume that there were several young boys under two years of age in the area, so the light was necessary to lead the wise men to the right house. The suggestion that the star was needed to guide them to Nazareth is not very convincing, since Matthew 2:11 says it was the house that was pointed out and not the town. Besides, why flee Nazareth?

Matthew's gospel says Joseph was visited in a dream by "the angel of the Lord" and ordered to "flee into Egypt" (Matthew 2:13-14). Immediately, Joseph awakened out of sleep, and gathered up the family and their belongings and fled to Egypt, leaving in the dark of the night. If they had been living in Nazareth and the slaughter of children was to take place in the area of Bethlehem, why would God send His angel to tell Joseph to flee Nazareth, even though Herod had jurisdiction there? It seems reasonable to conclude that the family was living in Bethlehem in the path of Herod's fury. The flight to Egypt was an absolute necessity for safety's sake.

There is another thing to consider. When Herod was dead, the angel of the Lord appeared again to Joseph in a dream and ordered him to return to Israel, (Matthew 2:19). Matthew 2:22 strongly implies that it was Joseph's intention to return to Bethlehem. If that is so, then it stands to reason that it must have been from Bethlehem that he fled, and not Nazareth. When Joseph learned that Herod's son Archelaus was ruling in place of his father, he was afraid to go to Bethlehem. There was no need for Joseph to fear if he was planning to live in Nazareth. He was warned in a dream not to go to Bethlehem so "he turned aside into the parts of Galilee" (Matthew 2:22). Why was there a need to warn Joseph against going to Bethlehem if he had no intention of going there? The

Lord knew exactly where Joseph was going and He changed Joseph's plans. The warning was necessary for by it, Joseph was "turned aside". Nazareth is in Galilee and Bethlehem is in Judea. It is at this point in the story where Luke 2:39 comes into the picture. "But when he heard that Archelaus did reign in Judaea in the room of his father Herod, he was afraid to go thither: notwithstanding, being warned of God in a dream, he turned aside into the parts of Galilee: And he came and dwelt in a city called Nazareth: that it might be fulfilled which was spoken by the prophets, He shall be called a Nazarene" (Matthew 2:22-23). "And when they had performed all things according to the law of the Lord, they returned into Galilee, to their own city Nazareth," (Luke 2:39), which they did after returning from Egypt.

Christ Was God's Answer

God is omniscient; He knows everything. He knows the future. He knew before Adam was created that Adam's race would need a Savior. He knew there would not be one sinner in all history who would be able to save himself from the wages of sin. In view of man's dilemma, the Godhead made a plan to save mankind. The plan was already in place the day Adam and Eve sinned against God. The plan was for God the Father to send His own Son into the world to die for the sins of all mankind. "And all that dwell upon the earth shall worship him, whose names are not written in the book of life of the Lamb, slain from the foundation of the world" (Revelation 13:8). It would take death to conquer death. "The wages of sin is death" (Romans 6:23) and Christ died and paid the wages of sin for every man. Based on Christ's death, God was then free to offer salvation to whosoever would receive salvation as a free gift.

Couldn't God have come up with another plan to save us? A better way or an easier way? If there had been a better way, that's the way God would have planned. God's way of solving the sin problem was the best way and has remained the only way. In the late 1800's and early 1900's the doctrines of the incarnation and Mary's virgin birth were challenged by unbelievers, agnostics, skeptics and those with limited understanding of the Scriptures. First, the godless unbelievers who never believed these doctrines rejected them because they reject God's supernatural acts. They try to explain everything in natural terms. Secondly, the religious entities who claim to believe them say these doctrines are not important. They often explain the Scriptures by distorting them. Thirdly, the mainline Protestant denominations said a person does not have to believe in the incarnation and virgin birth to be saved. These folks must have a lot of trouble with the passage in 1 John which says, "Hereby know ye the Spirit of God; every spirit that confesseth that Jesus Christ is come in the flesh is of God; And every spirit that confesseth not that Jesus Christ is come in the flesh is not of God: and this is that *spirit* of antichrist, whereof ye have heard that it should come; and even now is already in the world" (I John 4:2-3).

As these views became known, they brought two reactions. On the one hand, there were those who said it didn't matter what a person believed. This promoted indifference. The other reaction was to rise up in defense of the doctrine of the supernatural incarnation and the virgin birth, insisting that believing it mattered altogether. Reading through the Christian writings covering that period of time, it is quite noticeable that the writers did not rightly divide the Scriptures and thus mixed up some doctrines. One such example is confusing the Lord's appearing (commonly referred to as te Rapture) with the Second Coming of Christ.

Why did the incarnation and virgin birth take place? What was the purpose of God behind these two events? The Bible gives us clear answers and we do not have to guess or speculate about the reasons.

Sin means missing the mark, either deliberately or ignorantly. Either way, we all have missed the mark of God's will, purpose and righteousness. The Old Testament scapegoat is not a picture of atonement, but of sins being taken away, never to be recalled (Leviticus 16:8-26). Sins were lifted from the sinner and placed on the innocent goat. The goat was led into the wilderness and sent away, out of sight and presence, never to return or be seen again. There are people who are unconcerned about their sins. They deny them, excuse them or ignore them. But there are some who are in agony over their burden of sin. They acknowledge their sinful condition and loath it and hate every memory of sin. For those people there is wonderful news; great news. "Christ Jesus came into the world to save sinners" (2 Timothy 1:15). Some 2000 years ago "He appeared to put away sin by the sacrifice of Himself" (Hebrews 9:26). When He was born, His name was called Jesus for He shall save His people (Israel) and all who will receive Him as their only Savior, having taken away all their sins, yours and mine included. Praise His wonderful name.

CHAPTER 8

Peace on Earth

Peace on earth is a theme often seen on Christmas cards. It is the subject of many sermons during the Christmas season. Slogans and signs display the words "Peace On Earth". But, there is no peace on earth. The human race has never enjoyed peace because of sin. Sin causes mankind to be violent and rebellious.

In Luke we find a "multitude of the heavenly host saying (not singing), Glory to God in the highest, and on earth peace, good will toward men" (Luke 2:13-14). These are words inspired by the Holy Spirit of God. What was meant by this statement? A student pastor in a seminary was ridiculed by his professor for preaching about peace on earth because he saw no such thing. The student asked the professor if he had read the text carefully and went on to explain that though the English text reads "peace, good will toward men", the Greek text reads "peace on earth among those whom he has favored."[2] When men are favored, they do God's will, and then there is peace. When men seek to walk after their own will, they live in sin and there is no peace. Man is then opposed to God and often to other men. Man's ill will toward God and men makes peace impossible. The only place

---

[2] `Mounce, Wm & Robert Mounce, The Zondervan Greek and English Interlinear New Testament, Zondervan, Grand Rapids, MI, 2008.

in the world today where there is real peace is in the hearts of the believers in the Lord Jesus Christ.

The Bible speaks of different kinds of peace. Romans 5:1 speaks of "peace with God". Man, in his natural sinful condition, cannot be at peace with God. Because of sin, the sinner is estranged and separated from God. He has "sinned and come short of the glory of God" (Romans 3:23). There are no exceptions in time and history except the Lord Jesus Christ who knew no sin. All unbelieving sinners are separated from God and are doomed to pay the wages of sin, which is spiritual death; the sinner will be banished from God's presence forever. What a horrifying thought!

An unbelieving sinner has no relationship with God. What is worse, he cannot do anything to bring himself into a relationship with God. He is without hope, without the ability and the means to bridge the gap. Man cannot reconcile himself to God.

God knows man is incapable of reconciling himself to God, so, in His great mercy and love, God does everything necessary to reconcile man to Himself. He sent Christ into the world to give His life by dying and paying the wages of sin for all lost sinners. This is why Christ came into the world. God offers the free gift of salvation from the wages of sin by simply offering to any and all who will receive His gift of salvation by believing in the Lord Jesus Christ. Then, and only then, will man be reconciled to God.

Romans 3:10-16 describes the sinful ways in which unbelieving people live. Paul wrote "the way of peace they have not known" (Romans 3:17). People do not exercise good will toward each other. Peace is nearly unknown.

The Latin word *pax* means an agreement between two parties. It was a word used to describe a man and a woman who were about to be married. The Greek word for peace, *ierene,* means to reconcile, to bring back into harmony two who were in disagreement, or when one has offended another and brought discord. Often a moderator was involved to reconcile the two parties.

The basis for peace in the heart is belief in God. Sinners must respond to God's work of reconciliation. It is required that a person must believe in the Lord Jesus Christ for salvation. There is no other way for a man to be saved from the wages of sin and be reconciled to God.

Not only is there peace with God, there is the peace of God. "And the peace of God, which passeth all understanding, shall keep your hearts and minds through Christ Jesus" (Philippians 4:7). Nothing beats peace of mind. Peace of mind is a healthy spiritual condition. How can we have peace of mind? We must learn about the Lord Jesus Christ. Matthew wrote, "Take my yoke upon you, and learn of me; for I am meek and lowly in heart: and ye shall find rest unto your souls" (Matthew 11:29). The word "learn" is a mathematical term. A person comes to a conclusion after adding up all the facts and figuring them out. One learns of Christ, and the facts add up to the Son of God. He has the answers to life's problems. He has the answers to our questions. He gives peace of mind, rather than a troubled soul.

Mary's Song

The first chapter of the Gospel of Luke has three songs. We usually think of a song as a musical composition. But the Random House dictionary and Webster's dictionary give extensive meanings to the word *song*. They define it as a poetic composition. It does not have to be accompanied by music. Thus, we have in the Old Testament a book called the Song of Solomon or Song of Songs. It is a dramatic and lyrical love story of two married people who are in love which is credited to King Solomon. In the New Testament we have 1) Elisabeth's song (Luke 1:42-45). 2) Mary's song (Luke 1:46-55), and 3) Zacharias' song (Luke 1:67-79). Mary's song is often referred to as the Magnificat. The term is taken from the Greek words that mean *it magnifies*. To magnify is to make something larger in appearance than it really is for observation and learning. It can also mean to exaggerate. In Mary's song, it means to heighten by praising; to intensify the reality of the person and works of the Lord.

The background of Mary's song was her visit to her relative, Elisabeth, who lived outside of Nazareth in the hill country of Judea. It may have been not very far from Jerusalem since her husband, Zacharias, was a priest who officiated in the temple. Since Nazareth was in Galilee, this may have been a long journey for

Mary, the purpose of the visit was to share the news announced to her by the angel, Gabriel, who was sent by God to tell her she would be the mother of Israel's Messiah. The Messiah, she learned, would be the Son of God. Elisabeth was elderly and past the child bearing age, but had also supernaturally conceived a child and may have been about six months advanced in her pregnancy. The births of both of these children involved the supernatural, thus, they had something highly unusual and important to share with each other.

When Mary arrived at the house of Elisabeth, verse 41 says the baby in Elisabeth's womb leaped. The baby reacted to the voice of Mary. The Scriptures do not refer to this developing infant as a fetus, but as a baby. Fetus is a recent scientific term intended to misconstrue the definition of a baby to mean a stage of development of life in the womb before the baby is born, and not considered to be a human being yet. The Bible says differently. While in the womb, it is a human baby.

Luke 1:44 says the baby leaping was a reaction of joy. Can a fetus express joy? Verse 15 tells us a baby could respond with joy. The baby was already filled with the Holy Spirit of God, even before he was born. The baby whom Elisabeth was carrying had been supernaturally conceived, controlled by God's Spirit, who could leap for joy before being separated from his mother's womb. The fetus was a human baby.

What a joyful reunion the two women enjoyed. They were not only living on the threshold of one of history's greatest moments, they are also part of it, having been chosen by God. A detail that should not be overlooked is that Elisabeth already knew that Mary would conceive and bear this child, even before Mary's visit. Amazing! She addresses Mary upon her arrival as the "mother of my Lord" (Luke 1:43). In addition, Elisabeth knows that her own son is to be the forerunner of the Messiah. Her baby would be John the Baptist and his witness begins in the womb.

Mary's song was a response to Elisabeth's greeting. She says, "*my soul*". Soul has at least four meanings in the New Testament. In verse 46 it refers to the part of a person that perceives, reflects, feels, desires, wills and purposes. With perception and understanding, the sentiment expressed here by Mary's soul is praise. She knows very well what it means to become the mother of Israel's Savior. She was scarcely able to find words that express what this meant to her, and actually for all Israel. Her soul magnified the greatness of the Lord. Obviously, she was well acquainted with the Lord. To be so means she is well acquainted with the Scriptures of Moses and the Old Testament prophets. She knew the Lord and could not speak highly enough of Him.

Let's not stop here. In Luke we read that Mary says "My spirit hath rejoiced in God my Savior" (Luke1:47). The importance of these words should not be overlooked. Though others may disagree, her words imply Mary needed a Savior. She was a sinner like all other people on earth and needed to be saved from the wages of sin. If she had been born without sin, as some teach, she would not need a Savior.

Furthermore, there is not a single word in the Bible that she could or did save other people, or even help. The baby she would bear would be God in the flesh and her Savior. The word spirit has about eighteen different meanings in the Scriptures. Here, Mary's spirit was that inward part of her being that will live forever. She was alive and the life within her rejoiced with great joy.

Was Mary blessed above all other women? Not at all, nor does the Scriptures say so. What it says is *there*Nor does the Bible say she will bless others. Mary was blessed because of what God did, not because of what Mary did or because of who she was. If Mary was as well acquainted with the Old Testament, as it seems, then she may have known the following passages.

Isaiah 43:11, "I, even I, *am* the Lord; and beside me *there* is no savior".

Isaiah wrote, "Verily thou *art* a God that hidest thyself, O God of Israel, the Savior" (Isaiah 45:15). "But Israel shall be saved in the Lord with an everlasting salvation: ye shall not be ashamed nor confounded, world without end" (Isaiah 45:17). And verse 21, "Tell ye, and bring *them* near; yea, let them take counsel together: who hath declared this from ancient time? Who hath told it from that time? Have not I the Lord? And *there is* no God else beside me; a just God and a Savior; *there is* none beside me" (Isaiah 45:21).

Hosea 13:4,"Yet I *am* the Lord thy God from the land of Egypt, and thou shalt know no God but me: for *there is* no savior beside me."

From Luke 1:49, Mary gives credit where credit is due, namely, to the Lord and says "holy is His name". It is not Mary's name that is said to be holy, but the Lord's. Perhaps she knew Psalm 111:9, "He sent redemption unto His people: He hath commanded His covenant for ever: holy and reverend *is* His name."

Mary acknowledges God's mercy. Mercy is God's attitude of love in which he does for people what they cannot do for themselves. In Israel's infancy in the land of Egypt, they were helpless slaves. They needed deliverance but were unable to deliver themselves from the bondage forced upon them by the Egyptians. Mary knows that God's mercy "*is* on them that fear Him from generation to generation" (Luke 1:50). It never stops. Many people fear offending other people, but never worry about offending the Lord. Perhaps they think God cannot or refuses to be offended. God is offended by sin and hates it. "These six *things* doth the Lord hate: yea, seven *are* an abomination unto him: A proud look, a lying tongue, and hands that shed innocent blood, (like killing babies), an heart that deviseth wicked imaginations, feet that be swift in running to mischief, a false witness *that* speaketh lies, and he that soweth discord among brethren" (Proverbs 6:16-19). There is no fear of God in the minds of people who do these things. To those who do not fear the Lord, they refrain from such a lifestyle like that of Joseph and Mary who had lived godly lives in the fear of the Lord. Many Israelites traveling from Egypt to the promised land died in the wilderness because they did not fear the Lord.

In Luke 1:51, Mary says God "hath showed strength with his arm". Does God have arms? In men, power and strength is seen largely in their arms. In figurative language, God is said to have arms to describe His power and strength. Mary was a godly woman and well acquainted with the Scriptures. We know this because she quotes many Old Testament passages in her song. She most likely knew Psalm 89:10 and 13. "Thou hast broken Rahab in pieces, as one that is slain; thou hast scattered thine enemies with thy strong arm....Thou hast a mighty arm: strong is thy hand, *and* high is thy right hand" (Psalm 89:13 and 15). Mary's thoughts may go back to the Red Sea and the walls of Jericho when God showed His power and strength, both to the Gentile nations and to His people Israel.

Luke 1:52 expresses the thought that those invested with authority have this power invested in them by God. They are to govern for God but they rarely do because they are in rebellion against Him. Amaziah, 2 Chronicles 25:16, and Uzziah, 2 Chronicles. 26:20-21 are two cases in point. God dealt with both these men who rebelled against Him. In Daniel 5:20-30 we read of the Lord deposing kings Nebuchadnezzar and Belshazzar because they refused to acknowledge that Israel's God ruled the world as He pleased. Both were removed from their offices. Most likely Mary knew this and trusted God to govern her affairs according to His perfect will.

In Luke 1: 53 Mary praised God because He fills the hungry. Do the hungry know this? Do they praise the Lord as Mary did? Ingratitude is one of man's major shortcomings. It is a sin to be unthankful to the Lord. It was one of the major sins of the first families that peopled the earth. "Because that, when they knew God, they glorified *him* not as God, neither were thankful" (Romans1:21).

Luke 1:54-55 shows what Mary knew about the Bible. God's word was available to all Israel. The nation was without excuse for ignorance. God made many great promises to His people and fulfilled many of them. Any promises left unfulfilled will be fulfilled during the Tribulation and future Millennial kingdom.

Mary may have been a young girl, and she may have been poor for all we know, but she was godly and her song shows she knew her Bible. In the choice of a mother by whom the Lord would enter into the human race, God made a careful selection of a Mary. If He were to search the world today, would He find in Israel or the Gentile nations a woman who would qualify as a fitting mother for the Lord?

The Song of Zacharias

By New Testament times, the priesthood had grown to a very large number. Not all men in the tribe of Levi were qualified to serve or the number would have been even larger. The priesthood was divided into offices according to the work preformed. I Chronicles 24:1 begins "Now these are the divisions of the sons of Aaron" and then goes on in the rest of the chapter to name the men who were divided into 24 divisions. Zacharias was of one of these divisions called "the course, or division of Abia" (Luke 1:5). The duty of those of that course was to burn incense on the altar of incense in the sanctuary of the temple. In Zacharias's day, each priest served in the temple one seven-day week a year. In Luke 1:5-25 and 57-80 we have the record of the week of Zacharias's service. He did not live in Jerusalem. He lived in the hill country of Judea and made the journey into Jerusalem to fulfill his duties. On the first day of the week he assembled at the temple with the other priests for assignments. One priest, who was called the Officer, would cast lots to see who would get the temple chores. The first casting was for the cleaning and preparing of the brazen alter followed by sacrificial offerings. The second casting was for the cleaning and preparing of the candlestick and the cleaning of the altar of incense. The third casting was for the burning of the incense.

The priests of the family of Abia would stand in a circle. The Officer had pre-picked a number, so let's say the number was 148. He would begin to count as he went around the circle. The owner of finger 148 was the one who had the responsibility of burning the incense. For many priests it was a once in a lifetime opportunity to perform one of the most desired temple duties.

The burning of the incense in which the sweet-smelling smoke ascended and filled the room was symbolic of the prayers of the people of Israel. "Let my prayer be set forth before thee as incense; and the lifting up of my hands as the evening sacrifice" (Psalm 141:2).

On one particular day, the lot fell on Zacharias and it would be his duty to burn the incense. He would change from his street clothing into his priestly garments, as required, always made of fine white linen.

The priests milled around and visited and conversed with each other until the sun was about to rise. There were priests whose duty it was to blow trumpets. As soon as the first rays of the sun shined over Jerusalem, the trumpets would sound a three-fold blast. The priests hurried to their positions around the temple and the courtyard, and the people in the city were alerted that temple activities were about to begin. The first activity was for the priest who was burning incense that day to take two assistants and go to the east side of the brazen altar. One assistant would walk up the steps of the altar with a silver fire pan in his hand and scoop up a pan full of hot coals. He would carefully turn and descend the steps and pour the hot coals into a golden fire pan,

The three men walked around the altar to the west side until they were in front of the steps leading into the temple. Meanwhile, a crowd had formed outside the temple courtyard. Zacharias and his assistants would then walk up the twelve steps and pass through the first veil into the holy place called the sanctuary. The priests who had been working in the sanctuary would leave. The candles were lit and provided light. An assistant, who carried the hot coals would pour them on the altar of incense and immediately leave the sanctuary. Then Zacharias would scoop a bowl full of incense out of the incense bucket held by the other assistant who would also leave the sanctuary, and, as he emerged from behind the veil, this was the sign that all was ready. A trumpet sounded and the crowd would pray and Zacharias poured the bowl of incense on the hot coals. He prayed before the altar as the incense immediately began to burn and filled the room with the sweet odors rising up before the Lord.

Zacharias prayed and asked God for something. He asked for a son, for he and his wife Elisabeth were childless. Even though they were both old, he still asked.

On this particular morning an angel suddenly appeared and stood on the right side of the altar. His name was Gabriel and God sent him with a message. God had heard Zacharias's prayer and would grant his request (Luke, 1:11-13).

Zacharias was given specific information about his son. 1) He was to call his name John. 2) Many would rejoice at his birth. 3) He would be great in God's sight. 4) He would drink neither wine nor strong drink. 5) The son would be filled with God's Spirit and would have power like that of Elijah. 6) He would turn many people in Israel to God. 7) He would be the forerunner of the coming Messiah and prepare the way for Him.

Zacharias was very doubtful about all this so he was chastised with dumbness (perhaps deafness also) for a season. Outside, the crowd was waiting for Zacharias to emerge from the temple so they could be dismissed and wondering why it was taking him so long to come out. He finally appeared to give the benediction of Numbers 6:24-25 but was unable to speak. Perhaps another priest gave the benediction and the crowd dispersed, but they wondered what had happened to Zacharias (Luke 1:21-22).

The angel was right. Elisabeth conceived. When the child was born to this elderly couple, it was a matter of widespread interest, not because it had never happened before, for in fact it had (Abraham and Sarah), and that's just the point. When it happened in the past, it meant God was doing something special.

When the son was eight days old, he was circumcised according to the Mosaic Law. At this time, a Jewish boy received his name and it was almost always taken from a family member whom the parents wished to honor and remember. Many family and friends had gathered for this occasion. They were very surprised when they learned that the child's name would be John. They thought he should have been named after his father (Luke 1:61). When they appealed to Zacharias to see what he would say, he called for something on which to write and wrote, "his name is John" (Luke 1:63). This was a demonstration on the part of the parents of faith and obedience.

The people present were also very surprised when Zacharias spoke for the first time in nine months. His first words were a hymn of praise and assurance to God, (Luke 1:64-79). Zacharias was symbolic of all Israel. Both heard from God and both disbelieved. Both had lost sight of Messiah's coming. Both had been participating in Judaism, which had become burdened with ritual and unbelief. Both were chastised by God. Zacharias lost his speech and Israel lost her sight. God had silenced both because of unbelief. Faith and obedience opens the heart and loosens the tongue to praise God.

CHAPTER 9

Was Jesus Born on December 25?

Why is the date of the Lord Jesus' birth disputed? Everybody knows He was born on December 25. Or was He? In fact, the December date is highly questioned by Bible scholars and for good reasons.

Why do we even celebrate Christ's birth? The Bible does not teach us to do so. John the Baptist and the twelve disciples never mention it, and Paul, who wrote at least thirteen New Testament epistles never refers to Christ's day of birth. There is no known record that the first century church Christians ever observed it. How did it happen to become so widely acclaimed around the world?

Everything I have learned in life, it seems, I have learned from someone else. I have often wondered if I have ever had an original thought of my own, a thought no one on earth ever thought before me. I doubt it. I am indebted to my good friend, Pastor and Bible teacher, Richard Jordan, editor of the Grace Journal, who in turn was indebted to his friend and mentor, Clyde Reynolds, superintendent of the Mobile Rescue Mission, for guidance on the subject at hand.

Historians agree that the December date came to be chosen by apostate religion because the winter solstice began on December 25th according to the Julian calendar. The original Julian calendar had an eight-day week, but Julius Caesar had it revised by Roman and Greek mathematicians and astronomers to a seven-day week around 45 BC. After 500 AD Pope Gregory XIII had the calendar changed in which the winter solstice began on December 21. We now go by the Gregorian calendar. The solstice is the movement of the sun from north to south and vice versa. It reaches it southernmost point at 23.5 degrees on December 21 the shortest day of the year in the northern hemisphere, and begins its move north, each day getting longer until June 21, the longest day of the year.

Many dates have been suggested for the day of Jesus' birth, including January 6, March 25, April 9, May 20, and November 17, to name a few, according to the New Catholic Encyclopedia. Sun worship was common in the Roman Empire. The Persian god, Mithra, was proclaimed to be the principal patron of the empire and Mithra's birthday was celebrated on December 25. The Romans and Greeks called the celebration "the Nativity", meaning the nativity of the sun. It was celebrated with evergreens, wreaths, holly and mistletoe along with drinking toasts from wassail bowls (the forerunner of eggnog) and the exchanging of gifts.

Emperor Constantine brought December 25 into Christendom by naming Jesus instead of Mithra as the One to celebrate. All that the festival of the sun god's birth involved was transferred to the celebration of Jesus' birth. Thus, Christmas, literally, "Christ's mass", was adopted by the Roman church around the fifth to sixth century as part of Rome's consistent pattern of assimilating pagan religious ideas and making them part of life and worship.

If Jesus was not born on December 25, when was He born? It is widely accepted that we cannot know the date. Let us check the scriptural record carefully and see if a time of year can be discovered.

We must turn to the Gospel of Luke. Chapter 1 gives us many important details about the conception and birth of John the Baptist and Jesus. Luke is regarded by scholars as an exact historian, giving names of people, the times they lived and what they did. Luke's account in chapter one is further accepted for accuracy because every word Luke wrote was by divine inspiration. Chapter 1 is God breathed, so it can be trusted as an accurate guide.

Luke 1:5-17. Herod and Zacharias. Herod the Great was Rome's evil puppet king of Judea. Zacharias was a priest whose responsibility was that of burning incense in the temple of the Lord in Jerusalem. His office was called the course of Abia. In Luke chapter 1, Zacharias was in the temple carrying out his duties. It was while he was working that the angel, Gabriel, appeared to him with exciting news. His elderly wife, Elizabeth, who was barren and thus never bore him a child, was going to conceive and bear a son. The son would be a special child, great in the eyes of the Lord. The Lord would "go before him in the spirit and power of Elijah." "And many of the children of Israel shall he turn to the Lord their God" (Luke 1:15-17).

Luke 1:23-24. When Zacharias completed his term at the temple, he returned home. He lived in the hill country some distance from Jerusalem, perhaps thirty miles beyond the city. Upon arriving home, he had exciting news for Elizabeth, but there was a fly in the ointment. Zacharias did not believe the angel's message in the temple and therefore was struck with dumbness; he could not talk, (Luke 1:20). We do not know how he conveyed the angel's message to Elizabeth, but we can be sure he found a way and was quick about it. This news would have been too exciting to keep a minute longer. Elizabeth conceived shortly after Zacharias arrived home, and the baby grew to manhood and became known as John the Baptist, the prophesied forerunner of the Lord (Isaiah 40:3; Malachi 3:3; Matthew 3:3).

Luke 1:26-33. The scene shifts to Mary. Six months after the conception of John the Baptist, the angel, Gabriel, appeared to Mary in Nazareth to reveal that she would be the mother of Israel's long expected Messiah, who would sit on David's throne and govern as Israel's King. The angel told Mary she would conceive this child by the power of the Holy Spirit of God, (Luke 1:31). No human father would be involved. This had never happened before in the history of mankind. From this we understand that Jesus was conceived six months after John the Baptist, (Luke 1:36). Can the time of Elizabeth's conception of John the Baptist be fixed?

Remember that Zacharias was a priest after the order of Abia, (Luke 1:5 and 8). Luke says Zacharias executed his office before God "in the order of his course." When was he doing this? The answer is found in 1 Chronicles 24:10. The Greek word for the course is Abia; the Hebrew word for Abia is Abijah. In 1 Chronicles we learn that the arrangement of the priests in the temple was set by King David, (1 Chronicles 24:1). There were to be twenty-four courses, or "divisions", when each priestly family would serve in the temple. Each course lasted one week, from Sabbath to Sabbath, (2 Kings 11:9 and 2 Chronicles 23:4 and 8). Each priest would serve "in the order of his course" one week every six months.

All the men in Israel, including the priests, were required to go to Jerusalem for three major feasts, namely, Passover, Pentecost and the feast of Tabernacles, (Deuteronomy 16:16). That was the law. David instructed that a different order of priests would arrive at the temple each week between the feasts. Then, three times each year, all the priests served at the temple together during the three feasts.

When did Zacharias serve his course? 1 Chronicles 24:10 says the course of Abijah was the *eighth in order*. Eight weeks after Passover, beginning in mid April, puts the eighth course in the middle or late June. This would be when Zacharias was serving in the temple in Luke chapter 1, and it was at this time the angel appeared to him with the news of Elizabeth's soon conception of John the Baptist. After his service, he went home and Elizabeth conceived.

In the sixth month of Elizabeth's pregnancy, Mary conceived Jesus by the Holy Spirit. Since John the Baptist was conceived in June, his birth would have occurred in March the following year, 5 or 4 BC. Jesus was conceived six months after John the Baptist, so the conception would have taken placed in December, about the time of the winter solstice. This would place the birth of Jesus late in the month of September.

Is it important to know when Jesus was born? It might be a fact interesting to know, but not overly important. Then again, the Lord inspired Luke to record this information for a reason, so no one is out of order in learning it. Other things about Christ being born are far more important than the date.

CHAPTER 10

Was Mary the Mother of God?

Many people pray to God. There are also some who pray to Mary equally as much and perhaps even more. They pray to many saints, and Mary is regarded as the chief of saints.

All fundamental evangelical Christians believe in Mary, but they do not believe more than what the Scriptures ascribe to her. They believe 1) she was blessed by God to be the mother of Jesus. 2) She was holy, pure and good, 3) She conceived Jesus by the power of the Holy Spirit of God. 4) She was a virgin when Jesus was born.

What fundamental Christians do not believe is 1) She can hear prayers and/or answer them. 2) She is the chief of all saints. 3) She was conceived and born without a sin nature. 4) She never sinned. 5) She went directly to heaven after being raised from the dead. 6) She has any part in man's redemption. 7) She was ever in Rome. 8) She was the mother of God.

Mary was not without sin. In Paul's epistle to Timothy he says, "Knowing this, that the law is not made for a righteous man, but for the lawless and disobedient, for the ungodly and for sinners, for unholy and profane, for murderers of fathers and murderers of mothers, for manslayers" (I Timothy 1:9), and the list goes on. Mary was a law keeper, implying she was a sinner, or there would have been no need to keep the law. She made an offering to the

Lord for her purification after Jesus was born (Leviticus 12:1-6; Luke 2:21-24).

There are three positions held concerning the virgin birth of Christ. 1) It never happened because it is impossible, therefore it is denied. 2) The virgin birth happened but more is attributed to it than is attested to in the scripture. 3) The virgin birth is a fact of history but nothing more nor less is believed about it than what the scripture says. The third position is the safest because it has the least amount of argument and the most facts. It is solidly scriptural. How is it possible to have and to hold an adequate view of the Lord Jesus Christ if the virgin birth is denied or embellished beyond the facts stated in the Bible?

If the virgin birth is denied, the scriptures which attest to it are also denied, and this then leads to a greater problem, namely, how is it possible to trust the Bible as a whole if it cannot be trusted in part? Who would decide which parts are trustworthy and which are not, and on what basis?

To add more details to any scriptural account than what are stated in the Bible lends itself to no end of unrestrained ideas. It has been thought that in order to be the Lord's mother, Mary had to be born without sin and that God gave her a special pure soul. This is called the *immaculate conception*. It is further thought that Mary was taken to heaven after she died and was resurrected because she had no sin. This is called the *assumption*. It is also thought that after Christ was born, Mary remained a virgin and never had more children. This is called *perpetual viriginity*.

The Bible says "the wages of sin is death" (Romans 6:23). If Mary never sinned, why did she die?

The argument is that if Jesus was God, then Mary was the mother of God. But Jesus was God before He was born. His birth did not negate His deity. He remained as much God after He was born as He was in eternity past. In Isaiah's prophecy we read, "Therefore the Lord Himself shall give you a sign, Behold, a virgin shall conceive, and bear a son, and shall call His name Immanuel" (Isaiah 7:14). Matthew quotes Isaiah and gives the interpretation of the name Immanuel as "God with us" (Matthew 1:23). Luke says in his Gospel, "And the angel answered and said unto her, The Holy Ghost shall come upon thee, and the power of the Highest shall overshadow thee: therefore also that holy thing which shall be born of thee shall be called the Son of God" (Luke 1:35). Luke gives the account of Mary's visit to her relative Elisabeth who asked, "And whence is this to me, that the mother of my Lord should come to me?" (Luke 1:43). In view of these scriptural statements, was Mary the mother of God?

How can we justify denying Mary was the mother of God? First, God may be a singular noun in English, but that is not the case in Greek and Hebrew. The noun, God, refers to a plural Being. In Genesis 1:1, "In the beginning God...", the Hebrew word for God is plural. In Genesis 1:26-27, plural pronouns are used in reference to God; "let **us**"; "in **our** likeness". All three persons of the trinity were involved in the creation process. Is Mary the mother of the Father or the Holy Spirit who are God? She is the mother of neither. Is Mary the mother of God the Son? She is not. The Son was present in Genesis when creation was taking place and there are many passages of scripture that say so. Paul wrote, "All things were created by Him (Jesus) and for Him" (Colossians 1:16). John says "All things were made by Him, and without Him was not anything made that was made" (1 John 1:3). See also Ephesians 3:9, I Corinthians 8:6 and Revelations 4:11. Jesus Christ is the eternal Son of God and never had a beginning or a mother. To be the Son of God was understood to be God. "Therefore the Jews sought the more to kill Him, because He not only had broken the Sabbath, but said also that God was His Father, making Himself equal with God" (John 5:18). Mary was to give birth to Jesus, but without being the originator of His being or personality. Cf, I Timothy 2:13; Hebrews 10:5; I Corinthians 15:45; Colossians 2:9. Evan as God created Adam's body, with no genes being passed on to him, so was Christ's body created with no genes being passed on to Him. Jesus was the second Adam. It is correct to call Mary the mother of Jesus but with the understanding that His birth did not mark the beginning of His existence. Mary is never called the mother of God in the Bible. In fact, there are not very many references to her at all. Her name occurs just nineteen times, and the word *mother,* when it refers to her, just twenty-two times. Her name is found in Matthew, Mark and Luke and one time in Acts. John, who wrote five New Testament books never mentions

117

her name, nor does Paul, the apostle to the Gentile world. If James and Jude, who each wrote one book in the New Testament, were her sons, as some believe, it is strange that they never mention her even once. Peter, the leader of the twelve apostles, never mentions her in his two epistles.

Mary was truly a godly woman and should be respected as such. Luke 1:46-55 seems clear enough that she was probably a very young girl, perhaps not of the aristocracy of Israel, as though that would matter to the Lord. She was well versed in the Scriptures and acknowledged God's mercy, holiness and strength.

Mary should never be referred to today as the blessed virgin or the virgin Mary. She bore no such biblical title. She is so-called today because of the erroneous belief that she remained a virgin after Christ was born. The Bible presents an entirely different picture. In Matthew's Gospel it is stated that Joseph "knew her not *till* she had brought forth her firstborn son" (Matthew 1:25). The use of the word "till" implies that after Christ was born, the relationship between husband and wife changed. *Firstborn* means the first of two or more children. She and Joseph had at least four more sons and at least two daughters. The sons are named but daughters are not. There are at least eight references to the family of Joseph and Mary in the Gospels and Acts. When Jesus was preaching in Galilee, people were astonished at His profound teaching. It was not like that of the rabbinical teachers. It caused them to ask

118

in Matthew, "Is not this the carpenter's son? Is not his mother called Mary? And his brethren, James and Joses, and Simeon and Judas? And His sisters, are they not all with us?" (Matthew 13:55-56). To say that these men were relatives, cousins or nephews will not work. The Greek grammar and vocabulary will not permit it. Mary is to be respected as the mother of Jesus, not the blessed virgin or the mother of God.

We have as much respect for her as Jesus did, and as those who were around her, including the disciples. There is no record that she influenced the Lord during His earthly ministry, though there were perhaps times she may have attempted to do so. He did not need her help. Mary cannot intercede for anyone. She is not an intercessor or redeemer. She is not the mediator between God and man. Hebrews 7:25, 1 John 2:1-2 and 1 Timothy 2:5 make it quite clear that the Lord Jesus Christ is our Intercessor, Advocate and Mediator. Mary is not the hope of sinners. 1 Timothy 1:1 says the Lord Jesus Christ is our only hope. He is our everything. He is all we need. He is the light of the world, the way, the truth and the life. He is the only Savior of lost sinners. None of these things are said of Mary, nor does the Bible say anyone ever worshiped her or prayed to her. She calls the Lord her Savior in Luke 1:41 because she needed salvation like everyone else in Adam's race. It was a wonderful privilege for her to be the mother of Jesus, but in the end, it cost her a great price. A careful search of the scriptures and trust in its inspired words will separate fact from fiction. Religion is the storehouse of fiction;

Christianity is the guardian of the truth. The Church is the pillar and ground of the truth, (1 Timothy 3:15).

Philosophy, Rituals and Vain Worship

In Colossians 2, Paul taught the believers that they were complete in Christ. "For in Him dwelleth all the fullness of the Godhead bodily. And we are complete in him, which is the head of all principality and power" (Colossians 2:9-10). All that God requires of us for membership in the church that Paul calls the Body of Christ, and for citizenship in future heavenly places, has been fulfilled, accomplished, met and brought to realization in the Lord Jesus Christ. He has satisfied every demand of God the Father on our behalf. He, in His grace and mercy, did for us what we could never have done for ourselves. In Colossians Chapter 2 Paul admonishes, "Beware lest any man spoil you", verse 8. "Let no man therefore judge you", verse 16, "Let no man beguile you", verse 18. What did Paul mean by these three admonitions?

"Lest any man spoil you" (Colossians 2:8). He begins by saying, "beware". Every mail carrier and meter reader is well aware of what it means when they see a sign that says "Beware". It's a warning of danger. Here, Paul warns of dangers that cannot be seen with the eye. They are just as real and can be seen in the mind's eye. Six times in his epistles, Paul says, "Take heed". This does not mean proceed with caution, it means do not proceed at all.

120

Lest any man spoil you. Spoil does not mean to decay or rot, like an apple, nor turn sour like milk, nor use excessive indulgence like grandparents might do for grandchildren. It means booty, spoils, like the spoils of war. "To the victor belong the spoils" as the saying goes. This is a military term. Many soldiers have returned from the battle with souvenirs they brought back with them, mementos of their experiences. Spoils can also refer to people taken as prisoners. The point Paul is making is that he is warning people to beware lest they should be taken as prisoners of war in Satan's war of rebellion against God. Religion is a great deceiver and is soundly condemned in the Bible. The only belief systems God approved of were Judaism and Christianity. What tactics does Satan employ to capture the minds of believers? One tactic is human philosophy. Philosophy is imaginative thinking apart from God. It is sometimes disguised as being scriptural or spiritual. The Bible calls it man's wisdom. Man is in love with human wisdom. There was an attempt to replace Paul's gospel with philosophy. The function of the heart (the Bible word for the mind) is to think, reason, remember, learn, and understand. In our mind, we make choices. The problem is, our mind is influenced from within by our carnal nature, and from without by the world system which is controlled by Satan. We are bombarded with this influence all our waking hours. If the devil can cause a believer to think as the world thinks and act like the world acts, he can then destroy an effective testimony of a believer. There is a philosophy that is not after Christ. It leads away from Christ. The worst of all is religious philosophy. It is the opposite of Bible doctrine. This is a very real problem for Christians today. What's the answer? Don't make choices according to what the world thinks, but by what God thinks. Search the scriptures. His written word reveals His will.

The Cults and the Birth of Christ

Most cults object to the deity of Christ for two reasons. First, they say He could not be God and the Son of God at the same time. You cannot be the father of yourself. Second, they say that in the Bible the Father recognized Jesus as His Son, and Jesus recognized God as His Father. Therefore, the Bible implies that Jesus could not be God the Father, nor even God at all. This might sound like logical and sound reasoning but it isn't.

On the human level, we know that a person cannot be the father of one's own self. However, a man can be human and the son of a human. Christ can be God and the Son of God. His incarnation makes Him truly the unique man of history. His deity does not rest on man's logic or reasoning powers; it rests on God's word.

Christian Science believes that the idea of the incarnation was conceived by Mary, not God. It was Mary who named her son Jesus, God with us. Jesus, they teach, was the offspring of Mary's self-conscious communion with God. Jesus is an impersonal Savior, they say, and He is not God, but simply a divine ideal. Jesus is not Christ.

Spiritualism is the religion that deals with crystal balls, séances, cards and tea leaves, among other things. They teach that Jesus was only a medium of a higher order. Today, they say, we are taught by a spirit whose teachings supersede the teachings of Christ.

They deny the deity of Christ and say He never claimed to be God in the flesh. Jesus is now an advanced spirit in the 6th sphere. His claims of oneness with the Father are one of mediumship. Spiritualism had its beginning around 1848 in New York state. Some of it's most famous adherents were Arthur Conan Doyle and William James.

The Jehovah's Witnesses began around the 1870's with Charles Tate Russell, and at the first was called Russellism. He taught that before Jesus was born He was Michael the archangel, therefore He was a created angel and not co-eternal with God. He was not born truly and wholly man and God at the same time. In the flesh He lived a perfect life, but this was a purely human endeavor. He did better than anyone else.

Mormonism began with the teachings of Joseph Smith around 1830. This cult teaches that Jesus and Christ were two different individuals. (Other cults teach this also). They claim that Jesus was the offspring of Mary and Adam who was a god. But Christ was the offspring of David and Bathsheba, they say. If David had not been a polygamist, a redeemer would not have been born.

Unity School of Christianity was founded around 1889 and taught that anyone could adopt any religious belief they wished and it would be right. They believe that it is the will of God for all people to be healthy, wealthy and live peaceably with each other. They deny both the trinity and the deity of Christ. Founded by Mr. & Mrs. James Fillmore, it flourishes today.

Liberal Modern theology stands in sharp contrast to today's present fundamental, conservative, orthodox Christianity. Most of the mainstream Protestant denominational churches in America belong to this liberal group. Many of their ministers and teachers reject the incarnation; they also deny the deity of Christ and present Him as an idyllic figure. Some say He deluded His followers, including the twelve disciples, into thinking He was God. What harm would that be to them to believe that? Many say He was divine but so are we all. Everyone has a spark of divinity in them that needs only to be fanned. They teach that the Biblical records of the virgin birth are the products of men influenced by pagan fables and were not inspired by God or the Holy Spirit, and that belief in the virgin birth is not essential to Christian faith. Jesus was the master product of evolution.

Roman Catholicism teaches that Christ was born of a perfect sinless mother, Mary. She herself was conceived without sin (the immaculate conception). Being perfect, she gave birth to Jesus who is God; she is therefore the mother of God. God sent His only Son, Jesus Christ, to teach us how He wants us to worship God the Father. Jesus is the Son of God, the

Word, begotten of the Father in eternity before all time, having two nativities, one eternal with the Father, and the other in time of His mother. They teach that Christ is not the only Savior. Mary is referred to as Co-Redemptrix and we need her help to save ourselves by good works.

We must say at this point that we do not point out these differences in religious beliefs with any animosity. We believe they are wrong and have erred, not knowing or believing the words of the Scriptures. Errors need to be pointed out if they are to be corrected. Let us ask ourselves this question; why is there a denial of the biblical account of the incarnation? 1) Man is a truth rejecter. In Romans, Paul says, "Because that, when they knew God, they glorified *him* not as God, neither were thankful; but became vain in their imaginations, and their foolish heart was darkened. Professing themselves to be wise, they became fools, and changed the glory of the uncorruptible God into an image made like to corruptible man, and to birds, and fourfooted beasts, and creeping things" (Romans 1:21-23). And there it is. Man does not want to believe and obey the truth even when he knows it's the truth. He is ready to reject anything that is supernatural, therefore does not accept miracles as actual. That makes it easy to reject the miracles surrounding the supernatural conception and virgin birth of Christ. 2) Men are lovers and great admirers of their own good works. They think God is equally impressed. But Paul says in Ephesians that man is saved by His grace and man's faith which we get from knowing the Word of God, and that salvation is never by our good works, (Ephesians 2:8-9). Nor is the exercise of faith considered works. Salvation is a gift.

Many verses clearly teach the deity of Christ. "Who being in the form of God, thought it not robbery to be equal with God" (Philippians 2:6). "Jesus cried and said, He that believeth on me, believeth not on me, but on him that sent me. And he that seeth me seeth him that sent me" (John 12:44-45). "I and *my* Father are one" (John 10:30). "And we know that the Son of God is come, and hath given us an understanding, that we may know him that is true, and we are in him that is true, *even* in his Son Jesus Christ. This is the true God, and eternal life" (1 John 5:20). "In the beginning was the Word, and the Word was with God, and the Word was God. The same was in the beginning with God....And the Word (that was God) was made flesh, and dwelt among us, (and we beheld His glory, the glory as of the only begotten of the Father) full of grace and truth" (John 1:1-2 and 14). When Jesus was born, He was called Emmanuel which means "God with us" (Matthew 1:23).

Should Christians Observe Christmas?

Christmas, as it is observed by the unbelieving world, is filled with an abundance of nonsense. Imagine grown adults insisting 'Yes, Virginia, there is a Santa Claus'. Children are taught to believe Santa is an elf who has nine reindeer who have the amazing

126

ability to fly through the sky. One has an outstanding red nose that glows and can guide Santa and the other reindeer through the darkest night and worst weather. The reindeer pull a sleigh loaded with enough toys for all the good children in the world and they can be delivered in one night. Santa lives in the most inhospitable place on earth, the frigid north pole. He is married and has elves for helpers who manufacture toys in Santa's workshop. This ridiculous story is reinforced by taking children to visit a much larger Santa at the mall or department store to sit on his knee, telling him what they want for Christmas. If they can't make it to the mall, they can write Santa a letter with a list of the things they want for Christmas. These letters are actually mailed and go somewhere? Children leave Santa a snack on Christmas eve.

Added to all this is the religious element, some of which has its origins in paganism. When it is based on Scripture, it is often distorted and inaccurate. The Colossians lived in a pagan world and had much to distract them from Christian living. Paul has an important message for them, and his message is as pertinent today as it was when first given. The message is 'don't lose sight of the Lord Jesus Christ'. What, we might ask, would cause a believer to lose sight of the Lord Jesus Christ? Paul's answer. "the rudiments of the world" (Colossians 2:8).

One rudiment is human philosophy. Philosophy is a rationalizing of our existence and behavior. Most of the time it runs counter to God's truth. It's the opposite of the doctrines found in the Bible. For example, a God of love would never damn a soul to hell. The Bible says God will do exactly that. It is not His choice; man makes his own decision about where he will spend eternity. God does not overrule our choice.

Vain deceit is another rudiment of the world. Philosophy has to have a leader. Somewhere along the line there has to be a Plato or Socrates who are followed by others who accept their teachings. Men are very proud of their ideas that they consider original and worthy of acceptance. In their vanity, they want to be followed.

The traditions of men are another rudiment. They are practices developed which become the foundation upon which men build. Religion is full of tradition which has little or no basis in the Scriptures. Traditions are one of the hardest things to break because they are usually considered sacred.

The philosophies, vain deceits and traditions of the world system dominate the Christmas season and offer ample opportunity for the believer's mind to be turned away from Christ. How many believers do not go to church if Christmas is on a Sunday because they don't want to miss a football game, or are busy preparing a traditional Christmas dinner, exchanging gifts or visiting? There is no time for church or worship. How easy it is to lose sight of Christ at this time of the year.

Why December 25? It is not because Jesus was born on that day. Hardly anybody well versed in the Scriptures believes Christ's birth occurred on that day.

Many fine scholars believe He was born in the Spring or early summer. December 25 was a pagan holiday that had been celebrated hundreds of years before Jesus was born. It was dedicated to the god or gods who controlled the sun which reaches it's southernmost point at 23½ degrees south of the equator and begins at this point to move north again.

Christianity began in the first century with the preaching of the gospel but soon branched out in many directions and apostasy set in. About three hundred years after Jesus was born, a Roman emperor named Constantine declared Christianity the official state religion of his empire. At that time, the pagan traditions of the Romans were incorporated into Christianity. One tradition was the observance of December 25 as the birth date for Christ. In the beginning of the first century nobody observed Christ's birth. They did observe the time of Christ's death (1 Corinthians 11:26), but never His birth. As a result, the unbelieving world observes Christmas but not Christ's birth. If the truth will be admitted, they do not observe His death either. They have invented substitute reasons for these observances, like Santa Claus and Easter bunnies. They want no part of the Lord Jesus Christ. The worldly holiday music does not honor Him. The church hymns alone honor Christ.

In view of all this, what should be the attitude of the believer toward the Christmas season? Should we observe Christmas? First, we do not have to ignore it and we do not have to observe it like the world does. Second, the apostle Paul's admonition about avoiding the philosophies, vain thinking and traditions of unbelievers should help us to fix our eyes on Christ. The Christmas season gives the church a great opportunity to present the many truths about Christ's coming into the world. To all believers we suggest that if you want to observe Christmas, do not lose sight of the Lord Jesus Christ. Let His light shine through us before all, and especially before unbelievers in a world that is so dark with sin and ignorance who depend, unknowingly, upon our rock solid testimony.

"But after that the kindness and love of God our Savior toward man appeared, Not by works of righteousness which we have done, but according to his mercy he saved us, by the washing of regeneration, and renewing of the Holy Ghost; which he shed on us abundantly through Jesus Christ our Savior" (Titus 3:4-6).

www.ingramcontent.com/pod-product-compliance
Lightning Source LLC
LaVergne TN
LVHW021514080426
835509LV00018B/2507